DOVER

IN THE
SECOND WORLD WAR

Dunkirk survivors arrive at Dover.

DOVER

IN THE

SECOND WORLD WAR

Terry Sutton
and
Derek Leach

PHILLIMORE

First published 2010 by Phillimore & Co. Ltd
This paperback edition 2016

The History Press
The Mill, Brimscombe Port
Stroud, Gloucestershire, GL5 2QG
www.thehistorypress.co.uk

British Library Cataloguing in Publication Data.
A catalogue record for this book is available from the British Library.

ISBN 978 0 7509 6979 6

Typesetting and origination by The History Press
Printed in Great Britain

CONTENTS

LIST OF ILLUSTRATIONS

Frontispiece – Dunkirk survivors arrive at Dover.

Front endpaper: Sheltering in one of Dover's caves.

Rear endpaper: National Identity Card and evacuation notice.

ILLUSTRATION ACKNOWLEDGEMENTS

Bob Hollingsbee, 11, 16, 20, 24-6, 37, 39, 46, 54, 55, 59, 64, 74, 78, 82-3, 85-7, 96, 107, 109, 117-23, 125, 132; *Dover Express*, 18/endpaper, 36, 42-3, 47, 63, 75, 88-90, 92, 94, 102, 113; Dover Museum, 1 (d17412), 2 (d43771), 3 (d43689), 4 (do1890), 8 (d27064), 9 (d36590), 10 (do7491), 12 (d39775), 13 (d26043), 14/endpaper (d27620/d27621), 15 (d42391), 17 (d22237), 19 (do8980), 21 (d11636), 22 (do1095), 23 (d16767), 27 (do2932), 28 (do6154), 29 (do0088), 32 (d44270), 33 (do0266), 34 (do2955), 35 (do7457), 38 (do3100), 40 (do6059), 41 (do0581), 44 (d26509), 45 (d46055), 48 (do2958), 49 (d25328), 50 (d27836), 51 (d26307), 53 (do3104), 56 (do0303), 57 (d15617), 58 (d26753), 60 (do0099), 61 (do0254), 62 (do0261), 67 (d29944), 68 (d44290), 69 (d26310), 70 (d27826), 71 (d44272), 72 (do2747), 76 (d43275), 77 (d36609), 79 (d27686), 80 (d34814), 81 (d13199), 84 (d46063), 91 (do6350), 93 (d12964), 95 (do3001), 97 (d26300), 98 (d39765), 99 (d39913), 100 (do1739), 101 (d13841), 103 (d37991), 104 (d44043), 105 (d46010), 108 (d26503), 110 (d11643), 111 (d11644), 112 (d11654), 114 (d39911), 115 (d44292), 116 (do7512), 124 (do0567), 126 (do7551), 127 (d13193), 128 (d37885), 129 (d34799), 130 (d42373), 131 (d34811), 133 (d28990), 134 (d27670), 135 (d43452), 136 (do2929), 137 (do2931), 138 (d37997), 139 (do1226), 140 (d37998), 141 (d24979); Derek Leach, 6, 30; R.E. Puttee, 52, 73, 106; J.J. Smith, 7; Terry Sutton, 2, 31/endpaper, 65-6.

FOREWORD

EW TOWNS OF its size have suffered such punishment as Dover from bombing and shelling in the two world wars.

The first aerial bomb ever to crash down on the United Kingdom fell on Dover on Christmas Eve in 1914 and the last shell ever to hit the country exploded in Dover town centre in 1944. A further stick of bombs fell on Dover in 1945, but the RAF accidentally dropped them! They landed on Dover beach without causing any damage.

It is not surprising that Dover received so much attention from the enemy in both the 1914-18 war and the second conflict in 1939-45 because of its strategic position, just 21 miles from the continent. Dover has always been in the forefront of wars over the centuries, but never has Dover suffered so much as during the Second World War.

In the first, against the Kaiser's Germany, enemy warships shelled Dover although the 23 missiles that fell on the town did little damage. The fact, however, that German destroyers dared to enter the Strait caused considerable consternation.

The First World War was in its first year when a German aircraft dropped a high-explosive bomb on Dover, on Christmas Eve in 1914. It caused little damage, although it blew a gardener out of a tree where he was collecting Christmas decorations. The German pilot received a cash prize for his daring, a 'raid' depicted by enemy propaganda as a massive attack on Allied warships in the harbour. Another 183 bombs followed that single bomb in the next four years of war.

Dover, after hearing what happened in the Spanish civil war, knew what to expect in the way of enemy bombing when war was declared against Germany in 1939. Air-raid precautions had been in hand for at least 12 months.

What was not expected was that the German army in 1940 would scythe through France in a few weeks to end up on the French coast those 21 miles away. That gave the German gunners, with huge cross-Channel weapons, the opportunity to batter Dover by shellfire.

Records show that in the next four years 2,226 shells landed on the town of Dover with many more in the harbour waters, in the Dover Strait and in the nearby countryside. In addition to the shells (Dovorians never knew when the next one was coming), around 464 high explosive bombs, some 1,500 fire bombs, three highly damaging parachute mines and three V1 flying bombs dropped within the town's boundaries. No wonder Dover became known throughout the free world as 'Hellfire Corner'.

The population of Dover borough fell from 40,500 in early 1939 to an estimated 12,000 in 1940-1, before some of those who evacuated the town began to drift back. The town's population never fully recovered.

This book is dedicated to those people of Dover who 'stuck it out' for four long years, not knowing where the next high-explosive shell would land. It is written partly from Terry Sutton's own memories of the time, based on occasional visits to the town, and on the memories of others who, over the years, have told Terry, as a journalist, of their experiences in Britain's 'Front Line' town. A number of those, as the years roll by, are no longer with us. One who recently shared his memories died a few weeks later.

Greatly helpful, and an inspiration, were the war diaries and other papers kept by Norman Victor Sutton, who for much of the war was the only journalist (apart from his editor) working in the town throughout the bombardment. His memories of those terrible but exciting days resulted in the publication of a series of articles in the newspaper he later edited, the *Dover Express and East Kent News*. He was assisted in the compilation of those articles by his colleague Eddie Hollingsbee, whose son Bob is carrying on the tradition of garnering historical documents and photographs. Bob has greatly assisted in the provision of illustrations for this book, for which we thank him.

Terry Sutton and Derek Leach, 2010

1938

War Clouds over Europe

Prime Minister Neville Chamberlain came home from Munich in 1938 bearing a piece of paper that promised peace, but behind the scenes, Europe was preparing for war. For those who believed in portents there was a magnificent display at Dover of the Aurora Borealis, the Northern Lights, in January 1938 and a measurable earthquake in June.

In Dover rumours were rife about wooden pylons that were under construction at Swingate. When they were completed some claimed they were able to beam out a 'death ray', while more than one motorist swore their cars had suddenly ground to a halt on the Deal road near the Duke of York's Royal Military School, they claimed rays from the pylons were responsible. The authorities, knowing they were experimenting with radio location (later radar), did nothing to dispel those rumours. They might have even encouraged them. Later the wooden structures were replaced by four metal pylons, two of which remain to this day.

The town of Dover and its immediate hinterland was better prepared for war than most areas. For at least 12 months before the declaration of hostilities in September 1939, the borough council was preparing for war. There were those still in authority who were around in the 1914-18 war when German planes dropped bombs on the town and enemy destroyers in the English Channel shelled Dover. Members of Dover Borough Council seemed to be more aware of the dangers than those in authority at the Home Office and the Ministry of Health.

Early in 1938 there was a dispute between Dover and Whitehall over who should pay if there was a need for air-raid shelters. Dover, surrounded by chalk hills and cliffs, enjoyed the benefit of a number of caves, some of which had been used as shelters during the First World War. The town council wanted to extend these as air-raid shelters, but Whitehall, at that stage, refused to pay the substantial grant requested by Dover, expressing the view that officials would prefer to rely on the individual Anderson shelters that were to be provided, if necessary.

1 Swingate steel pylons that replaced the wooden structures.

The town council had begun to enrol volunteers for air-raid duties in 1937, following a mass meeting at the Town Hall addressed by a Home Office minister. The council then set up a Dover & District Air Raid Precautions (ARP) Committee (under the ARP Act of 1937).

Early in 1938 this committee considered how to carry out anti-gas training and was told that 38 members of the council's staff, nearly 50 members of the St John Ambulance Brigade together with a score of employees of Dover Harbour Board were undergoing training at Dover Isolation Hospital at Noah's Ark Road. Gas masks for civilians were to be stored in St James's Boys' School. During the same month the Home Office informed Dover

2 Isolation and Eye Hospital.

council that they would be expected to get involved in a national ARP publicity campaign, including the establishment of a new organisation for women – the Women's Voluntary Service (WVS) – to help with ARP arrangements. It was also reported to the committee that Mr Sutton, Dover Harbour Board's works superintendent, was making arrangements for the deployment of auxiliary fire pumps.

In various parts of the town, including Pencester Gardens, gangs of men began digging trenches where people could shelter from the shrapnel from anti-aircraft fire. Neighbours at the top of Stanhope Road grouped together and began digging an E-shaped trench that was to be covered with corrugated iron in the vain hope of providing shelter. Children mixed with the men, helping in the digging, but were probably more of a hindrance than a help. The men, some of whom had wartime experience of slit trench warfare in Flanders in the 1914-18 war, managed to complete the main backbone of the shelter, but by the time the crisis ended little progress had been made on the arms of the E-shaped shelter.

3   *Old Park mansion.*

4   *Dover Harbour in 1939.*

Mr Chamberlain's 'peace in our time' declaration was made, and so the diggers all went home. Remains of that weed-covered shelter can still be found today in the field at the top of Stanhope Road.

One great fear in 1938 was that if war broke out, poison gas would be used against civilians. To combat this threat a Gas Officer was appointed to train volunteers for anti-gas duties. Woodland's store in Bridge Street was purchased by the council as a centre where gas masks could be kept and fitted. In fact, gas masks did not arrive in the town until late September, but the fire station in Ladywell had been open for people to be measured for the masks that smelt of rubber.

There were, however, those who refused to believe that war was possible, with one councillor during a debate describing fears about an outbreak of hostilities as 'Tommy rot.'

Two local companies of the Territorials were mobilised and, according to the *Dover Express*, 'made a magnificent response to the call to arms.' In March it was revealed by the government that the War Department had bought Old Park estate from Mr Murray Lawes, where modern barracks were to be built. In the harbour there was more evidence of the Royal Navy and there was talk of the formation of a new Dover Patrol, which had proved so valuable in the First World War. Later in the year, as Austria was annexed into the German Reich and, in September, Czechoslovakia fell, there was another crisis before the Munich agreement relieved the growing tension once again. At the year's end there was much nervousness but, at least, the nation was still at peace.

1939

'Consequently we are at War'

THROUGHOUT THE LAST months of peace, Dover was preparing for the threatened conflict ahead. Barry Fincham, now living at River, remembers:

With my sister we used to watch soldiers camouflaging themselves in hedgerows all out around our locality where we were then living. We watched tank traps under construction along the railway lines and with concrete obstacles at the bottom of Crabble Hill, near where is now the Daihatsu garage. I remember earning rebukes from my father as he struggled to erect the Anderson shelter in our back garden. That first siren frightened all of us and we took shelter in the next door neighbour's wooden garden shed!

The clash of views with Whitehall continued in April 1939 when the Home Office decided Dover was to be a reception area for evacuees from vulnerable towns if it should come to war. Dover Rural Council was to prepare to accommodate 2,000 children from the Medway area of Kent. Official records show that the town and village representatives rejected the idea, explaining there were 'difficulties'. These included the expected exodus of town residents migrating to neighbouring villages to avoid enemy bombing. After much debate and a visit by a delegation from the two councils to Whitehall, the Home Office accepted Dover's argument and made it a 'neutral' area with no evacuees arriving or departing. In just over 12 months, however, Dover and the villages did become an evacuation area.

Preparing for the worst the authorities ordered air-raid siren tests in February and July, but in August the mayor, pub landlord Jimmy Cairns, warned that the next time the sirens were heard it would be for real. Sandbags were prepared for the protection of historic buildings and for use to dampen firebombs if dropped on the town.

Another worrying decision was to remove the stained glass windows from the ancient Maison Dieu Hall at the Town Hall to safety in tunnels under Dover Castle where they remained for about eight years.

5   *Seafront defences in 1939.*

As August drifted towards September and the threat of war grew, hundreds of holidaymakers from the continent, including Germany, began arriving at the western docks and Marine Station. Also packing the departing trains were the tourists who, in normal numbers, had been spending a few days in Dover. Everyone was going home.

As the expectation of conflict grew there was a rush by housewives to buy thick material to cover windows in case the government ordered a general 'blackout' at night when no light was allowed to be seen from houses. Many windows were criss-crossed with sticky paper to prevent the splintering of glass.

In September 1939, as tension rose, Dover Borough Council was locked in conflict with the Home Office over who should pay for converting a large water tunnel on Dover hills into an air-raid shelter. The cost was reported to be £4,385. The scheme, which was implemented, was to widen the water main tunnel running from Noah's Ark Road to Union Road (later Coombe Valley Road) and to link it with Edred Road and Widred Road. Later, the council voted to send a letter of thanks to a group of volunteers who excavated an entrance to the water main tunnel shelter at the top of Edred Road.

Mr Chamberlain announced a change in compulsory military service with the age limits extended from 18 to forty-one. At the same time the Italian government declared that Italy would take no initiatives in military operations.

On 1 September 1939 Germany invaded Poland, resulting in Britain and France declaring a general mobilisation. Prime Minister Neville Chamberlain warned the German government that unless their forces were promptly withdrawn from Polish territory, the British would fulfil its obligations to Poland.

Then on Sunday 3 September came the dramatic broadcast on the wireless by Prime Minister Neville Chamberlain that Germany had refused to withdraw its invading troops from Poland, and 'consequently Britain was at war with Germany'. The King also broadcast to his people, urging them to stand 'calm, firm and united'.

6   *St Mary's Church.*

Minutes after the prime minister's broadcast the air-raid sirens were wailing as an unidentified aircraft was seen approaching the coast. It turned out to be a friendly aircraft flying in from France but the sound of that first siren was terrifying, with expectations of seeing squadrons of enemy bombers sweeping in from over the hills at any minute.

The war announcement came as a large congregation prayed for peace at the town's civic church, St Mary-the-Virgin. John Lockyer, now living in Hove in Sussex, was a young choirboy at the morning service and recalls how the congregation was informed. A sidesman walked up the central aisle of the church and handed a note to the vicar. He read it and indicated to the organist to pause in his playing. Lockyer recalls:

> The vicar then delivered the terrible news that Great Britain was 'now at war' with Germany. When the sirens sounded shortly afterwards only a few of the congregation stirred from their pews. When the service ended, probably shortened, the young choristers were advised by the vicar to hurry home.

Another young lad in the choir was John J. Smith, aged 10. He remembers that morning service well. He remembers:

> Soon after eleven that morning the siren sounded, indicating an air raid was imminent. There was a hush among the congregation and then my father appeared at the side door of the church with both his and my gas mask. We hurried home to Stembrook as fast as our legs would take us and made straight for our air-raid shelter only to find it ankle deep in water. We all were under the impression that a gas attack was being launched.

There was no need to worry on this occasion and the All Clear was sounded shortly afterwards.

Allan Edgington, a young schoolboy, had accompanied his younger brothers to the Methodist Church Sunday School and when that finished he was about to go to the Methodist Church at the corner of Beaconsfield Road.

> It was suggested that something important was about to happen and I was advised to take my brothers home. We got as far as Shatterlocks field (off Buckland Avenue) when the siren went. We were halfway across the field and we ran home like scared rabbits.

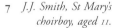

7   *J.J. Smith, St Mary's choirboy, aged 11.*

8   *Waldershare Park.*

In the first days of the war thousands of soldiers were drafted into Dover. There were so many there was not sufficient military accommodation for them so the army began billeting them in civilian homes. We had three Royal Artillery gunners allocated to us. Each time the siren went at that stage in the war they had to parade further along the road. I often wonder if those three soldiers survived the war and what happened to them.

Journalist Norman Sutton noted in his 'war diary' that Dover cricket week was cancelled and the West Indians, due to play at Canterbury, sailed for home. His diary continued:

Guards have been mounted at the railway stations and at other places. ARP workers and troops around the port. Military lorries everywhere. More destroyers and trawlers arrive in the harbour. Hospital patients evacuated to Waldershare on Friday.

This reference to the evacuation of hospital patients followed an invitation from Lord and Lady Guilford for the patients at Dover's Royal Victoria Hospital and the nursing staff to leave the town centre and move out to their mansion home on the Waldershare Estate. They went and remained there for six years before returning to the main street hospital, now converted into flats.

The outbreak of war also resulted in a rush to acquire gas masks, which were fitted at Dover fire station in Ladywell. From then on, at least for a few months, no one went out

9   *Gas mask drill.*

without their gas mask in its provided box, slung from the shoulder. A general blackout was imposed and householders got into trouble if any lights were visible from a property.

Walter Bates, aged eight in 1939, remembers the Anderson shelters being delivered. He recalls:

> I asked my father why big sections of rounded metal were being delivered to every home along the street and why big holes were being dug in the gardens. He explained we were at war and the rounded metal were parts of air-raid shelters for our safety. Neighbours all pitched in together and, in amazing quick time, these shelters were assembled. They were to provide fun, in the early part of the war, for us youngsters but the dank smell in them was awful.

At the Eastern Docks, then back under Admiralty control, mining work was in progress constructing huge underground storage containers inside the cliffs for fuel oil that would be required by the Royal Navy. Vice Admiral Bertram Ramsay, later to be the main architect for the Dunkirk evacuation, took command of the Royal Navy's Dover station. He was no stranger to Dover, having commanded the destroyer HMS *Broke* in the First World War.

With the declaration of war several rights of way near military installations were closed to the public, including paths near Dover Castle. In peacetime these were favourite Sunday afternoon walks for many Dovorians.

Many more troops began arriving in Dover in September 1939, among them were militia called up under the National Service Act. They were joined by scores of reservists. Some were billeted at River and Buckland. The Black Watch, headed by their band, marched from their barracks to the railway station. They were soon to be despatched with the British Expeditionary Force (BEF) to France. Local members of the 'Terriers', serving in the 75th (Cinque Ports) Heavy Anti-Aircraft Regiment were given the task of defending the town against air attacks. Their guns were deployed at Swingate, Guston, St Radigund's, Langdon, Farthingloe and even on Dover seafront.

In the early days of the war there was not much for the troops to do in their spare time. It was a boom time for many of Dover's public houses, although there was often a shortage of beer! The navy boys took over several pubs, including those in the Market Square, while the troops congregated in other establishments.

Despite the strict 'blackout' there were often queues outside Dover's four cinemas and those who got inside to watch the films could return again free if their entertainment was halted by a raid threatening the premises. Some watching *Gone With The Wind* at The Granada in Castle Street returned several times because of interruptions by the enemy.

There were more false air-raid siren alarms in September and, on 6 September, anti-aircraft guns were in action against an unidentified aircraft.

It was not long before the town's cinemas, closed with the threat of war, re-opened and were soon crowded with soldiers, sailors and civilians. Football matches were allowed to restart on 14 October.

Dover's civilian ferry links with the continent were suspended and the ships switched to Folkestone. No ship was permitted to enter Dover harbour without express permission.

10   *Sitting upon an Anderson shelter.*

11   *Ack-ack installations.*

12   *The Granada Cinema, Castle Street.*

There was plenty of activity at Dover docks, with the train ferries being repainted grey and being immediately brought into use laying mines in and around the Dover Strait in the hope of blocking the passage of enemy submarines.

On shore it was what many elsewhere described as the 'phoney war', but that was not so at sea. In his diary, Norman Sutton records that the 530-ton HMS *Kittiwake*, a patrol vessel of the First Anti-Submarine Flotilla, struck a mine shortly after leaving Dover harbour. Five members of the crew were killed and, according to the journalist, the badly damaged warship berthed in the Camber at the Eastern Docks. The dead were the first to be accommodated in Dover's war mortuary.

A sea mine was washed up just east of the Eastern Arm of the harbour during a gale. It exploded, smashing a few windows at East Cliff.

There were reports in the town that three enemy submarines (U-boats) had been sunk in and around the Dover Strait. At least one was off the port and four dead German submariners were brought to Dover and placed in the town's mortuary. Others who were injured were treated at Deal while some were made prisoners of war. The funeral of the four dead Germans took place quietly at St James' cemetery on 17 October and was delayed for

13   *Dover-Dunkirk train ferry.*

an hour by an air-raid warning. Later, with so many air-raid warnings, funerals continued even during enemy shelling.

One of the time-consuming chores for many households in Dover was putting up window shutters at dusk and taking them down again in the morning. Experience showed that the glass in windows was less likely to shatter from bomb and shell blast if protected by shutters. This gave rise to many taking up the DIY task of making shutters that could be slipped into place over windows. This also helped meet the blackout regulations. The shutters were normally made of a wooden frame that held tarpaulin in place.

The government provision of Anderson shelters was speeded up in Dover and families were busy digging them into their back gardens. Preparations were also made in October for the introduction of rationing. Every household in Dover had to fill in a form giving details of all the people in residence. From these details identity cards were issued shortly after.

In November 1939, a public meeting was held at Dover Town Hall where the speakers, including a representative of the Ministry of Agriculture, explained the need to grow-your-own because merchant ships were required to import other commodities. The town clerk, backing up the guest speaker, said there were allotments available in the town, but added a list of sites where, if required, more garden plots could be made available. The meeting agreed to set up a Dig for Victory committee.

On the 'home front' life remained fairly quiet, but not at sea from where there were often explosions as ships were mined. Enemy seaplanes were busy landing in the English Channel

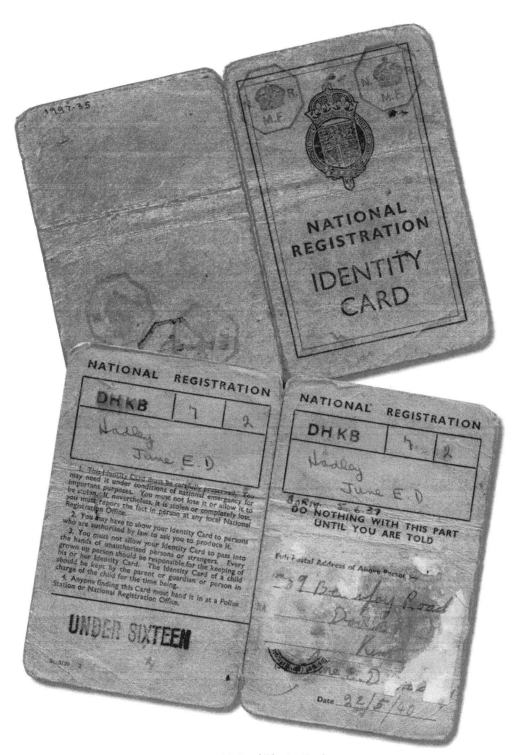

14 *National Identity Card.*

15   Victoria Park.

sewing magnetic mines that resulted in the sinking of a number of ships, including vessels belonging to neutral countries.

Many of the houses in Dover's Victoria Park, once the homes of senior army officers, were requisitioned to accommodate Royal Navy officers and members of the Women's Royal Naval Service (WRNS).

One German submarine, attempting to escape the Royal Navy, ran onto the Goodwin Sands off Deal. The Dover lifeboat, later to be withdrawn from service, ventured out to the Goodwins, but it was reported the submarine was a complete wreck and it was quickly sucked down into the sands. There was something strange about this incident. Five bodies of the German submariners were washed up between Hythe and Rye some time later. But there were about 10 days unaccounted for between the submarine going on the Goodwins and, according to the medical evidence, the date of the death of the Germans. Where had they been those ten days?

Meanwhile, at Dover docks there was feverish activity placing electric 'degaussing' apparatus around ships, a method that was successfully deployed to beat the magnetic mine menace.

16   *Drifter minesweepers in the harbour.*

17   Lord Warden Hotel.

There was excitement in the town in December, just before Christmas, when an anti-aircraft shell fired accidentally from the docks and struck a tree in Cherry Tree Avenue. No one was hurt and only slight damage occurred.

A few days before Christmas soldiers from the BEF began returning from France for festive leave. Some of them were accommodated in the *Lord Warden Hotel* at the western docks and at the Oil Mills then in Limekiln Street (now the site of Hammond's fuel-filling station).

And so 1939 ended fairly peacefully.

1940

Battle of Britain

I N THOSE EARLY dark months of 1940 more people were to die falling into the blacked-out docks than from enemy action. The black-out, when no lights were permitted to be seen from houses and street lights were turned off, had been in force for months and more than a hundred people had been fined in Dover for failing to enforce the restrictions. The blackout resulted in a series of fatal accidents on Dover's roads and at the unfenced docks. The *Dover Express* reported how, during the early wartime years, some seafarers fell into the docks but were rescued by colleagues; others were not so lucky and drowned.

The coroner, Mr E.T. Lambert, at the inquest of one of the first Dover civilians to be run down by a vehicle during the blackout observed: 'I am afraid this is one of the first of what I expect will be a number of inquests because of the need to black out the highways.'

A few weeks later a different coroner, Mr J.B. Robin, conducted an inquest on a Royal Navy chief petty officer killed by a train at the blacked-out Marine Station. He commented that no blame could be attached to the train driver and blamed the blackout conditions.

Mr Lambert was called in again to investigate the death, in the Granville Dock, of Derek Manton, a 51-year-old labourer of Dover's Beach Street. The evidence given was that Mr Manton, working in a lit workshop on the quayside, came out into the complete darkness and, temporarily blinded, just walked off the quay into the dock where he drowned. 'It's to the discredit of the blackout', said Mr Lambert, recording a verdict of misadventure.

Investigating the death of Ernest Lucas, serving in the navy, who fell into the dock and was drowned, Mr Lambert commented: 'This is the fourth or fifth case I have had to consider of death caused in this way in the blackout.' A Royal Navy officer told the coroner that something should be done to alleviate the danger and suggested the dock should be fenced. The coroner, recording another misadventure verdict, agreed, saying: 'It would certainly help if guard rails were put in place around the docks. Otherwise I doubt if this will be the last case of its kind before me.' Following the coroner's remarks the docks were then fenced, which not only helped safety, but also increased security where Royal Navy ships were berthed.

Rationing of food – butter, sugar and bacon – began on 8 January and was to continue in some form or other long after the war had ended.

A mine in the Downs off Deal sank the liner *Dunbar Castle*, a regular caller at the port in peacetime. A female passenger was landed at Dover but died shortly afterwards in hospital. On 11 January two German Dornier aircraft flew over Dover at around 20,000 feet when there was anti-aircraft fire, while at sea ships continued to be sunk by mines. On 11 March a Blenheim, operating with anti-aircraft gunners on an exercise, crashed near St Margaret's when it hit a tree. A Welsh Guards officer on the aircraft was killed.

In many ways Dover was fortunate, surrounded by chalk hills, to have scores of caves where men, women and children sheltered during the worst of the bombing and shelling. In the early days of 1940, Dover's town clerk, Sidney Loxton, asked the *Dover Express* to publish a full list of the 59 cave shelters, trenches, basements and school shelters in the town. The list included the maximum number of people who could shelter in the places. There was also a reminder that the 18 school shelters mentioned could not be

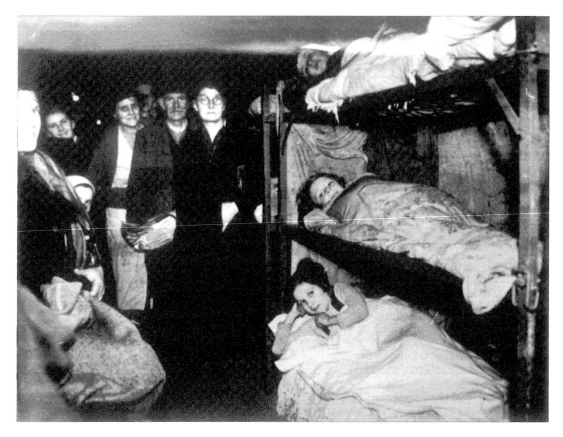

18   *Sheltering in one of Dover's caves.*

19   *Brewing tea underground.*

used while children were at school but could be used during school holidays and on Saturdays and Sundays.

The biggest cave shelter was the long tunnel from Winchelsea to Priory Hill which, according to the newspaper advertisement, could accommodate 1,400 people. This proved to be one of the most popular shelters in Dover.

Other cave shelters were at Athol Terrace, the Chapel Cave at East Cliff (185 people), Trevanion Street cave (behind what is now the sports centre), Barwick's cave in Snargate Street, the bonded store in Limekiln Street (known by some as the Champagne Cave), one in the bank opposite Laureston Place, room for 200 in the chalk bank beside the Regent cinema in London Road (now the army recruiting centre), Lagoon Cave running underground from the High Street to Tower Hamlets Road, and a cave at Chapel Hill that could take 100 people.

There were trenches available in Pencester Gardens, Dover College playing field at Elms Vale (now a residential area), in Union Road (now Coombe Valley Road), Connaught Park which offered shelter for 423 people, at Shatterlocks off Heathfield Avenue and in Barton Road.

There were also 16 so-called basement shelters in the premises of local businesses where people could dash into in the event of a raid. One of the most popular was in the basement of Fremlin's Brewery in heavily bombed St James' Lane. Even Woolworths in Biggin Street offered shelter for 300 in its basement.

One shelter that was often used during shelling raids was the railway arch between Buckland Church Path and St Andrew's Terrace, which was protected at each end by sandbagged hoardings.

The King visited Dover twice in the early months of the year to inspect ships and the troops. On 11 April Prime Minister Neville Chamberlain resigned and Winston Churchill took his place.

There was little enemy air activity and the sirens were not sounded very often in those early months of the year, but on 3 May an enemy plane on reconnaissance was over the town and on the same night there was plenty of mine-laying off Dover in the path of the military leave ships.

An RAF Hurricane, just sent to a base in France, attacked German fighters and during the mêlée the pilot ran out of fuel. He turned towards the coast, lost his way and baled out near the Swingate masts. He was unhurt but his aircraft was lost.

About this time the first enemy bombs of the war were dropped on English soil. They fell in a wood near Chilham.

The Ostend ferries ceased sailing on 7 May, and three days later the Germans invaded Holland and Belgium.

Norman Sutton, a Dover journalist, in his diary records:

I went for a walk on the cliffs towards St Margaret's Bay and was surprised to see people using binoculars which I thought were prohibited. On May 11 blockades erected on roads into Dover, the same day a Spitfire crashed on the St Margaret's road, the following day went to Deal and saw a number of wrecks in the sea.
  On the 14th May a number of German prisoners were landed at Dover as well as wounded from a destroyer. On the 15th I interviewed, and took the names of a number of parashots. On the 17th May Dutch soldiers march through the town together with British sailors in French uniforms, understood to be from HMS *Valentine*.

The balloon was about to go up (to use 1940s jargon) with increased air activity over the town resulting in, for the first time, the firing of additional anti-aircraft guns recently installed, including some on the promenade.

Winston Churchill ordered roadblocks to be set up just in case the Germans should suddenly invade. People entering Dover on main roads had to establish their identities.

Secretly, a detachment of Royal Marines passed through Dover to embark on a destroyer for Holland and they covered the evacuation of the Queen of the Netherlands and her government, who arrived at Dover on the steamer *Maid of Orleans*. It is believed they brought with them much of the gold held in Dutch government banks.

One of those who helped in the reception of the refugees was bus driver Joe Harman. He told, long before he died, of how on 22 May he backed an East Kent bus along the length of the Prince of Wales Pier, expecting a Stuka attack at any time:

When we reached the pier head we saw a small fishing boat disgorging their human cargo of men, women and children. We ferried them to Dover's town hall to sort out the categories for onward movement. A check was made on them all in case they were fifth-columnists. One was sent to Pentonville.

He also told the drama, and other wartime action, in his autobiography, *My Dover.*

That day, 22 May, a Junkers 88 was seen off Dover heading towards the town. It was attacked and shot down by the famous Squadron Leader Malan. The three Germans were killed.

Three days later, in sight of Dover, two Hurricanes collided in mid-air and were reported missing. The next day a Spitfire crash-landed on the beach at Deal when its engine failed after shooting down an enemy Junkers aircraft. The Hornchurch pilot of the Spitfire had a bullet in his knee. On 27 May an RAF Hector, operating with Lysanders dropping supplies to the besieged British forces in Calais, crashed near Shakespeare Cliff on its way back to base.

Within a fortnight of the attack on Holland, the enemy was on the French coast at Calais. Dover from now on, for four long years, was the nation's front line.

The RAF sent in Blenheims during the fighting around Dunkirk and several were shot down by the Luftwaffe. One came down near the Goodwin Sands, another near St Margaret's Bay with a third in the sea off Dover.

Norman Sutton was mixing with Fleet Street journalists at the *Grand Hotel* and elsewhere and knew more about what was going on with the BEF in France than most Dovorians. It was a strange situation at *The Grand*, where local people and visitors still drank their gin and tonics while early survivors dropped in for a rest. Naval officers, survivors from a sunken destroyer, called in still covered in oil. There were all sorts of rumours about the retreat across the Channel of Allied forces.

It was enough for Norman Sutton to pack his wife and son off to relatives in the Medway Towns which, for a small boy, was the start of years of evacuation, trailing from Sevenoaks to mining villages in South Wales and eventually to the steelworks town of Ebbw Vale.

With Dover in the front line in 1940, and expecting a German invasion, a scheme of voluntary evacuation of school children was implemented. This was in marked contrast to an earlier decision by the government, later rescinded, to make Dover a reception area for evacuated children from London and other cities. All this changed on 26 May when parents were invited to register their children of school age for evacuation. No destination was given.

On Sunday 2 June, 2,899 Dover children were marched from their schools, with their teachers, to the Priory Station where special trains were waiting. Parents had been banned from the railway station to prevent upsetting scenes for the children. John J. Smith remembers that day well:

> It was about the same time that the soldiers were being evacuated from Dunkirk. We saw the troop trains travelling through with soldiers looking dishevelled and tired. Our school assembled at our school in Queen Street and we had been told to bring clothing and our gas masks. We were given labels with our names and details on and taken to the railway

station. There were hundreds of children with their teachers boarding trains to somewhere. To where we just did not know. But many hours later we finished up in a town called Blaenavon in the Rhondda Valley in South Wales.

The house of the lady who took me in was very old and we had to draw water from an outside tap. Sheep used to come round to the door. The lady had three children of her own including a daughter, aged about 15. When we had a bath it was in a long tin bath in front of the fire. It was at this stage I discovered boys were different from girls.

The children, with their schools, went to different towns in Monmouthshire, South Wales. The towns where they ended up, although not even the teachers knew where they were heading, included Blackwood, Ynysddu, Pontllanfraith, Cwmbran, Blaenavon, Risca, Caerleon, Ebbw Vale and even Severn Tunnel Junction.

Most of the evacuated children were treated well by their Welsh foster parents, but a few were soon writing home pleading with their parents to return to Dover. Bob Cain, billeted with one family, told this story:

My foster mother believed someone had stolen a slice of bread. It was mid-winter with thick snow on the ground, but she made us stand in the garden in our pyjamas for hours until one of the other evacuees confessed he had eaten it.

Bob later moved to Ebbw Vale, to Dover County School, where he had much better treatment.

20   *Evacuees leaving Dover for Wales.*

21-2   Evacuees leaving Dover.

Not all Dover boys and girls opted for evacuation, which was not compulsory. Some parents refused to allow their children to go off into the unknown. Those who remained in Dover had no schooling for around 18 months and came to be known in national newspapers as Dover's 'dead end kids'. Barry Fincham was one of those left behind. He recalls:

> With no schools there was plenty of time to watch barrage balloons and searchlights being installed. The one in Cherry Tree Avenue (now Kwikfit garage) was one of my favourite places when getting the groceries from the Co-Operative Store. Part-time schooling commenced in 1942 at Buckland School with boys in the morning and girls in the afternoon. Dover's population almost halved and so I knew practically everyone in our locality.

Some children were evacuated privately and then returned to Dover. One was Maurice Amos who remembers:

> I was sent to relatives in Plymouth, just as the bombing of the docks there began. So after three weeks I was brought back to my home in Buckland Avenue, Dover. No schools were

23   *Vice Admiral Bertram Ramsay – mastermind of the Dunkirk evacuation.*

open at that stage but two ladies (who I think were German Jewish) opened a small private school at Rosemount near Whitfield Church and I went there until the local authority schools opened again. But we could then only attend part-time as there was not sufficient room for us all in the air-raid shelters for a full complement of boys. So one week we went in the mornings and the next week in the afternoons. It was great fun, looking back, but very dangerous too.

Very soon, as factories and shops closed down, many of those living in Dover decided to move to somewhere safer and, it was estimated, during 1940-1 the town's population fell to 12,000 – the lowest it had been for hundreds of years.

During the ferocious fighting at Calais, Boulogne and at Dunkirk, gunfire could be heard all day at Dover and on 26 May the so-called army parashots, trained to kill enemy paratroopers, went on duty in and around Dover.

The next day a plane crashed at Aycliffe and the authorities decided school children at Dover would be evacuated. All schools were closed. Barry Fincham recalls:

The schools closed and there was talk of invasion. Many of my friends were evacuated. My mother told us we must all stay together when the Germans came and not to be afraid. I remember being taken to Dover's evacuated hospital at Waldershare Park for tonsil extraction. There were wounded soldiers everywhere so I was sent home straight away after the operation because every bed was required. When would the dreaded Germans come?

The story of the evacuation of 338,000 British and French troops from Dunkirk has been told many times. The majority of them, 202,300, were landed at Dover's western docks where they were checked before scores of trains carried them inland from the Marine Station. A large number of the French soldiers evacuated from Dunkirk by the British later returned to join the French army in the south of their country. Dover people volunteered to man feeding stations and First Aid posts for the returning troops.

Buckland Hospital in Union Road (now Coombe Valley Road) was never busier than during the Dunkirk evacuation when hundreds of badly injured soldiers and sailors, landed at the Admiralty Pier, were taken by ambulances to the surgery theatres. Dr Gertrude Toland FRCS, a Dover general practitioner, was one of the leading surgeons working many hours non-stop. One of the surprises at the end of the war was that Dr Toland never received any official recognition.

Former British Rail and Sealink shore staff say they remember the quayside buildings alongside the train ferry dock at Dover still had walls marked out designating the area where the dead, taken from the ships returning from the Dunkirk evacuation, were to be stacked.

So many wounded BEF soldiers were dying on the homecoming ships that the authorities realised they had to buried somewhere. In July 1940 Dover Borough Council received a request from the War Graves Commission to be allowed to erect temporary wooden crosses at the mass graves being dug at the town-owned St James' cemetery. The council agreed to

24   *British troops arriving at the Western Docks from Dunkirk.*

25   *Dunkirk survivors arrive at Admiralty Pier.*

26   *Allied troops from Dunkirk arrive at Dover.*

27   *Dunkirk survivors arrive at Dover.*

28   *Dunkirk survivors arrive at Dover.*

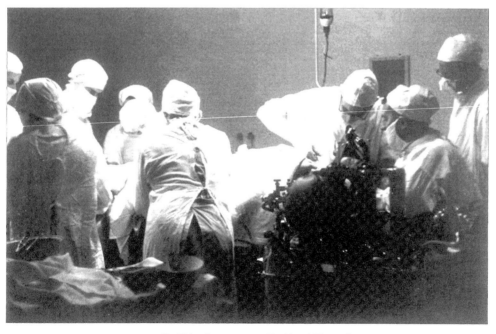

29   *Dr Toland operating at Buckland Hospital.*

30   *Second World War remains of 355 servicemen buried at St James' Cemetery.*

the request which included a promise that, in time, the wooden crosses would be replaced with the normal type of headstone.

The Royal Navy was busy, among other duties, picking up pilots out of the sea. One rescue, at the end of May, was of two members of the crew of a Defiant that ditched in the Dover Strait. It had fought and shot down a Heinkel 111 but return fire had filled the cockpit with smoke.

Norman Sutton recorded:

> Following the Dunkirk evacuation, completed on June 3rd, it was quiet in Dover until June 16th when France capitulated. There were then sirens on the 18th, 19th, two on the 22nd, 24th and two again on the 25th.

On 3 July, he recorded, there was a battle between fighters over Dover and two days later six bombs were dropped in an attempt to hit ships in the harbour. One of the raiders was brought down.

After the Dunkirk evacuation scores of civilians moved out of Dover to places of greater safety. Dover's civilian population plummeted so much that town councillors expressed fears that the town and its remaining shopkeepers would go bankrupt. The town clerk took advertising space in the *Dover Express* to remind those evacuating that they still had to pay

IMPORTANT NOTICE

EVACUATION

The public throughout the country generally are being told to " stay put " in the event of invasion. For military reasons, however, it will in the event of attack be necessary to remove from this town all except those persons who have been specially instructed to stay. An order for the compulsory evacuation of this town will be given when in the judgment of the Government it is necessary, and plans have been arranged to give effect to such an order when it is made.

You will wish to know how you can help NOW in these plans.

THOSE WHO ARE ENGAGED IN WORK OF ANY DESCRIPTION IN THE TOWN SHOULD STAY FOR THE PRESENT.

OTHER PERSONS SHOULD, SO FAR AS THEY ARE ABLE TO DO SO, MAKE ARRANGEMENTS TO LEAVE THE TOWN—PARTICULARLY

MOTHERS WITH YOUNG CHILDREN
SCHOOL CHILDREN
AGED AND INFIRM PERSONS
PERSONS WITHOUT OCCUPATION OR IN
RETIREMENT.

All such persons who can arrange for their accommodation with relatives or friends in some other part of the country should do so. Assistance for railway fares and accommodation will be given to those who require it.

Advice and, where possible, assistance will be given to persons who desire to leave the town but are unable to make their own arrangements.

Information about these matters can be obtained from the local Council Offices.

(Signed) AUCKLAND GEDDES,
Regional Commissioner for Civil Defence.

TUNBRIDGE WELLS,
2nd July, 1940.

(393/4177A) Wt. 19544 30 70M 7/40 H & S Ltd. Gp. 393

their landlords rent until the end of their lease and, more importantly as far as the council was concerned, rates still had to be paid.

The bombing attacks on Dover began in earnest in July 1940. The month was six days old when 10 bombs fell around the Coombe Valley and Buckland. On 7 July there was a big battle over Dover with three German aircraft brought down, while a Spitfire crashed at Hougham. On that day more bombs were dropped on shipping in the harbour. On the following day German raiders were over Dover again with more bombs dropped, some by dive-bombing Junkers aircraft. A Spitfire was brought down and crashed in flames near Green Lane, Temple Ewell.

Walter Nicholl of Shepherdswell remembers well the 1940 air attacks, one while he was working in his father's bakery at Elms Vale:

> Many of my pals had been evacuated but my father, also Walter and a master baker, was short of staff because his workers had been called up. I was 13 and he decided I should remain in Dover and help him. One day there was an air-raid and my mother suggested we close the shop and go in the air-raid shelter. There were two customers in the shop and after they had left, the shop was closed. There was an explosion and the shop was hit. There was flour everywhere. The man who had been in the shop was still outside. We thought he had fallen asleep. But, no, he was dead. I remember there was a cottage loaf beside him.

Day after day, German bombers and fighters were over Dover, the harbour and the Strait as the Luftwaffe tried to eliminate the RAF before the launch of an invasion of Britain. On 14 July Stuka dive bombers attacked shipping off Dover. HMS *Vanessa* was hit by bombs and towed into Dover harbour by the port's tug, *Lady Duncannon*.

One raid, not very successful, was carried out by planes of the Italian air force, shortly after Italy joined Germany in the war in order to grab a share of defeated France. The old-fashioned Italian Fiat aircraft took off from near the Belgian border, ran into heavy anti-aircraft fire over Dover, jettisoned bombs and speedily made off. They never returned to Dover and it was suggested the Germans had allowed the raid to give the Italian pilots a bit of practice.

Later in the year an Italian squadron was attacked by the RAF off Folkestone when 10 of the Corpo Aereo Italiano aircraft were shot down. By 1941 the Germans had sent all the Italian pilots back home because of poor training, inadequate aircraft and lack of experience.

In July a German air-sea rescue seaplane was captured near the Goodwin Sands. Both the British and the Germans made great efforts to save their pilots down in the sea, partly in order so they could fight again. On this occasion the RAF's 54 Squadron fliers forced down the German seaplane, near the Goodwins, and the enemy crew were made prisoners of war. A trawler towed the Boulogne-based seaplane inshore to near Deal and the following day the aircraft was towed to Dover harbour. But the very next day the seaplane was destroyed in an enemy attack.

The BBC and other media sent reporters to Dover to describe the attacks on Channel shipping and the early days of the Battle of Britain. German and British aircraft were being brought down and crashing in fields and, on occasion, on homes. A Bolton Paul Defiant crashed at Elms Vale. Damaged planes, both German and British, trailing smoke and parachutes descending, became regular sights in Dover.

The 20 July German attack on the harbour was successful in that the Admiralty tanker *War Sepoy* was so badly damaged it broke its back. It was later towed to the harbour entrance and sunk as a blockship to prevent enemy submarines penetrating the harbour.

On 24 July there was a heavy attack on a convoy passing through the Dover Strait but no ships were hit. There was a more successful attack on a convoy the following day when four ships were sunk and one was so badly damaged it had to be beached below Shakespeare Cliff. During this air attack enemy E-boats tried to intervene and were driven off by destroyers. It was claimed some 400 aircraft, Allied and German, were involved in this battle.

The following day HMS *Codrington* was hit by a bomb and sank alongside the Eastern Arm. Later the bows of the ship were towed to Dover beach where, for months after the war, it was used (dangerously) by children as a diving board.

On 28 July there was another dogfight when a Hornchurch-based Spitfire was shot down by a German fighter. People in the Buckland area watched it falling until it crashed onto the roof of Buckland Mill. The badly injured pilot, Sergeant Eric Mould, was seen coming down by parachute to land safely near Bunkers Hill.

Walter Bates remembers the time well. He recalls:

> By 1940, when things were really bad, we would go to the Winchelsea area caves for shelter. These caves ran from Winchelsea chalk pit through to the top of Priory Hill while there was an offshoot tunnel that ran to the back of Westmount College in Folkestone Road. These caves, dug out of solid chalk, proved very much a lifesaver over the coming years. Inside the caves there were bunk beds on one side and bench seats on the other, lighted with dull electric lights. But there was no heating.

When his own school was damaged in one attack, and he had to move to another, Walter used to use the caves as a short cut, to save climbing over the hills.

The most furious air attack on Dover harbour came on 29 July when 30 dive bombers escorted by 50 fighters roared in from the Channel at breakfast time. For 10 minutes the noise was terrific as bombs rained down on navy ships moored at the Eastern Arm. The enemy planes flew so low that soldiers stationed on harbour installations took pot shots with their rifles. Messerschmitts, Spitfires and Hurricanes were crashing in the sea throughout the day. Coastguards reported three aircraft down in the sea off Folkestone but the would-be rescuers found only scraps of Luftwaffe uniforms. The RAF came to the rescue of the ships in the harbour and by the time the sudden attack was over the enemy had lost a fifth of their planes. But the damage was done. The Royal Navy's depot ship HMS *Sandhurst* was ablaze and the wreck of HMS *Codrington* alongside it was further damaged. Dover firemen fought the blaze on *Sandhurst* all day, ignoring the large amount of ammunition and torpedoes on the ship, resting in a sea of oil that was on fire. For their bravery three Dover firemen, Ernest Harmer, Cyril Brown and Alex Campbell, received the George Cross while five others received commendations.

Soon after this attack, when other ships were badly damaged, the Royal Navy pulled most of its larger warships out of Dover.

This attack spurred on the authorities to provide increased defences for the port and town and the first of more than a score of silver-coloured barrage balloons arrived. This provided German fighter pilots with a bit of fun in hit-and-run visits to Dover to shoot down the barrage balloons. It also gave the less experienced Luftwaffe pilots a lesson in shooting practice.

32 Sandhurst *and* Codrington *hit in Dover Harbour.*

George Barton, before he died, told his local newspaper how in 1940 he was 'spotting' for the Dover Fire Service:

> I recollect I was posted as lookout atop of the ancient Constable's Tower in Dover Castle and watching, in low cloud, Messerschmitt fighters swooping down on barrage balloons to shoot them down in flames through the murk. My job was to estimate the areas of the fall of the balloon for the fire station. All this while bullets were thudding into the walls of the tower below.

Balloon sites were at the boys' grammar school fields at Astor Avenue, Granville Gardens, Aycliffe, Cherry Tree Avenue, Connaught Park, the grounds of Dover College and the college's cricket ground off Folkestone Road.

The barrage balloon crews were kept busy, hauling down their silvery monsters before they were shot down in flames and when there were lightning storms that also struck. Whenever there was a storm Dover people used to rush to the window to see if the crews could bring their balloons back to earth before they came down in flames following an electric storm strike.

33 *Barrage balloon in Dover Harbour.*

One national newspaper pictured a balloon falling earthwards in flames and wrongly captioned the photograph claiming it was an enemy aircraft, possibly a government-sourced propaganda picture. It is claimed that one balloon crew, based at the Granville Gardens on the seafront, brought down a Messerschmitt 109 by rifle fire.

Ken Flint, now living in Deal, was a soldier based in requisitioned accommodation in Crabble Avenue and he remembers the kindness shown to him and his comrades:

34 *Barrage balloon on fire.*

I recall that the railway arch at the end of Crabble Avenue was adapted as a shelter from the bombing and shelling. Both ends were partially barricaded with sandbags while benches were provided for those taking shelter. During one prolonged shelling raid I was sitting there when I noticed two girls who were obviously not at all frightened by the shelling. This resulted in a long friendship between them and me and one of my pals.

Ken Flint was stationed during the worst of the Hellfire Corner days in the underground tunnels beneath Dover Castle, the headquarters of Admiral Ramsay. In these various layers of tunnels, army, navy and air force personnel collected detailed information about attacks and convoy movements in a communications centre and sent their messages to various headquarters. One tunnel was set up as a first-aid hospital where a number of injured air crew and naval personnel were treated. But the underground hospital was not as busy as expected. There was also barrack accommodation under Dover's white cliffs.

These balloon-potting incidents were designed by the German high command to try to force the RAF into action, shoot the British down and win command of the air. It was the start of the Battle of Britain. The enemy knew that the RAF had to be destroyed before they could launch any invasion.

In the first phase of the massive air battles, for 10 days the Germans concentrated upon attacking shipping in the Dover Strait, on harbours and RAF fighter bases. German and British fighters were shot down during these fights over Dover with several crashing in fields around the town. A Spitfire, on convoy escort duties, was shot down and crashed near the Dover-Deal road. Another six Spitfires were shot down or were forced to crash land, one near Kingsdown where Pilot Officer Finney was killed.

Walter Bates, again:

We watched the Battle of Britain start. As children we were fascinated by the battles of the airplanes above our heads. We would hang on the wall at the end of Percival Terrace and wonder at the white streaks in the sky and listen to the rat-a-tat tat of the machine guns and cannon fire up in the sky. Dover was becoming known as Hellfire Corner, and not without good reason.

35 *Underground barracks in the White Cliffs.*

Another Dover resident at the time was Derek Friend. In a Kent County Council publication, *The Field of Human Conflict* (1990), he said:

I'll always remember watching the dog fights during that long hot summer, the white contrails twisting and turning, sometimes ending in a long black, fiery streak falling to earth and then parachutes drifting down.

In the first week of the Battle of Britain the Dover sirens sounded 20 times. The bombs dropped on Dover at this stage were still on the light side. But the government was fully aware of the danger of invasion and of the threat to life in Dover and other coastal towns. Dover and Folkestone were declared a Defence Area and made subject to compulsory evacuation if required.

This led to a debate in Dover council chamber, reported in the *Dover Express* and copied many times by authors of books on the war. During the debate Dover's mayor, Jimmy Cairns, pleaded with the town's citizens to stay put if possible, pointing out that bankruptcy would face the town if everyone departed and trade dried up.

Sir Aukland Geddes, the government-appointed Regional Commissioner for the South East, contacted the town council and suggested it should nominate nine councillors out of the 24 to stay behind in Dover in the event of an invasion. That idea, according to the newspaper report, was rejected, with Councillor John Walker exclaiming: 'What would the Empire think if Dover Council did not stand firm?' A few months later Councillor Walker, aged 54, was killed by enemy action on Dover seafront while tending his boats.

Aircraft, British and German, continued to be shot down around Dover in August with a Spitfire forced down at Capel and another at West Langdon. The pilot baled out but died of his injuries. A Gravesend-based Hurricane came down at Alkham, but the pilot who baled out was unhurt.

In the same month Pilot Officer Peter Stevenson, flying a Spitfire, had a terrible experience. His aircraft was shot down by cannon fire and he was dragged from the cockpit when he opened the canopy. His leg became entangled with the shrouds of his parachute and when he fell into the sea he was unable to cut himself clear. The 'chute then dragged him with his head under the water for several minutes. He was in the sea for about an hour before being picked up by a Motor Torpedo Boat (MTB).

On 1 September the Royal Observer Corps reported the wave of bombers and fighters passing over Dover was five miles long, on the way to attack RAF airfields and London docks. One German fighter, based at Amiens, was brought down and crashed near St Radigund's Abbey. The crew members were made prisoners of war.

At 11 a.m. on 12 August, a new danger appeared for the people of Dover. It was the first day a German shell, fired from the French coast, hit the town. It destroyed four houses in Edgar Crescent, off what is now Coombe Valley Road. At first it could not be understood how there were explosions with no enemy aircraft about. But checks on the remains of shell casing confirmed they had been fired by long-range guns. Norman Sutton's war diary records:

This day [12 August] we had five sirens and shellfire. Two killed at St Radigund's and other damage at Noah's Ark Road, Edgar Crescent, and at Minnis Lane. Further attacks every day [from 12 August to 22 August]. On [the] 15th the electricity grid lines were smashed and the cut lasted for nearly 11 hours. On the 19th there was no siren sounded but seven bombs, including one that killed 14 soldiers at a football match. On 22 August there was more shelling when St Barnabus Church hit, others in Maison Dieu Road and at River.

Reginald Foster was sent to Dover by his newspaper, the *Daily Herald*, and he described in his book *Dover Front*, published in 1941, details about the first shells:

It is probable that for some time the enemy were using French long-range guns transported from the Maginot Line on their specially constructed railway trucks. Fragments and parts of shells with French markings have been found.

Notices were put up on boards on the approach roads to Dover when there were raids. They either said: 'The town is being shelled' or: 'Air raid in progress'. These warnings were designed for military drivers because very few civilians could get petrol to fuel their vehicles.

36   *German propaganda photograph of a cross-Channel gun at Calais.*

37   *Folkestone Road damage.*

Dover Isolation Hospital at Noah's Ark Road (now the site of the Ark church) was closed in the autumn because of the danger of raids and the patients were transferred to Ashford, at the cost to Dover ratepayers of 12s. 6d. per person per day. The hospital buildings were then earmarked as a reserve casualty centre in the event of mass deaths as a result of enemy action.

Maurice Amos of Brookfield Place, Dover, recalls:

Shelling started in 1940 and the shells came without warning. This began the onslaught that continued for four years. As time went on a new method of warning was devised instead of the normal air-raid warnings. The new system provided a one minute siren warning, then

38   *Air-raid warning notice.*

© Illustrated, from Black Star

Nazi Bombs Often Change Dover Bus Routes, So Warning and Queue Signs Must Be Mobile

During air raids, or shelling, people waiting in line for buses often hold their places instead of seeking shelter. No one may take advantage of confusion at such times to "crash" the queue—it is against the law.

39   *Bus diversions due to shelling.*

a gap, then another one minute warning. The idea was to give warning of an expected shelling raid and allowed us to take shelter   hopefully. Then, an hour after the last shell fell (again hopefully) the All Clear would sound.

After a time people had to just grin and bear it and started to try to live as normally as they could, dodging into the shelters that were provided here and there. One was under the railway arch at Crabble and in various caves. Loudspeakers were installed on the lamp posts in the main street which were used to give instructions. The loudspeakers told people to take cover and were used to officially announce the capture of the German guns in France that had been shelling Dover. That was a cheering announcement.

When the shelling was intense we could obtain basic rations from a warden's post at Buckland Bridge. That occurred during the last month of shelling (September 1944) when we lived most of the day in our Anderson shelter. I had already slept in that Anderson shelter for four years. What days they were.

The number of Police War Reserve officers in Dover was increased from 31 to 65 to deal with air-raid incidents and possible looting.

Allan Edgington recalls that his father, at home in Knights Way, used to stand in the bedroom window and on a clear night would be able to see the flashes of the guns on the French coast and give early warning of a shell arriving.

Norman Sutton's diary adds that a British Blenheim, returning from a bombing raid, struck a barrage balloon cable and fell on the Chevalier Road, home of popular police constable William Maycock, killing him and his wife Mary. The aircraft's crew of three also died. The officer and his wife left two children, aged five and two years, and the local council granted an allowance to them of £15 each a year.

This was a terrible time for Dover with attacks from the air virtually daily, sirens several times a day and shells crashing down on Dover homes. The number of Dovorians killed and injured was begin to mount up.

Walter Bates, like many others, was spending more time sheltering in the caves. He says:

I spent many happy hours in the caves while the war went on outside. People died, some with terrible injuries but life went on, day after day, night after night. Being young one seems to adapt to unbelievable conditions. Many of the men would stand and smoke in the entrance to the caves but this was dangerous.

The Regional Controller of the Civil Defence based at Tunbridge Wells contacted Dover's town clerk by telegram in August 1940 to say the Home Office had decided to impose a 10.30 p.m. curfew along a coastal belt that included

Dover. A year later this was relaxed to 11 p.m. Nobody was supposed to be out after that time except to save lives or to further the war effort. As part of the curfew 'places of public resort', including public houses, had to close by 10.30 p.m. Police records show that Dover's chief constable, Marshall Bolt, had in July 1940 suggested a 10 p.m. curfew, but, following a letter from the Royal Navy's Flag Officer at Dover Castle, special arrangements were made to permit access to the *Lord Warden Hotel*, used by the navy.

Another regulation imposed on the coastal belt from Margate to Hythe, and five miles inland, was that no private cars or motor cycles were allowed on the streets without a special police permit. Owners were instructed to immobilise their vehicles and take the removed parts to the nearest police station.

In September life was getting so dangerous in Dover that at the town council meeting Councillor Jim Ryeland proposed that the Regional Controller be asked to consider a scheme for the compulsory evacuation from Dover of all non-essential residents. The idea was overwhelmingly rejected by three votes to 13 with Mayor Jimmy Cairns abstaining. Those who voted in favour were Mr Ryeland, Aldermen Powell and Norman. A month later the council was told that a resident of Folkestone Road had written to the mayor complaining about the decision.

Pregnant women were, however, evacuated. The council was informed in September that 37 had been removed under a government scheme for expectant mothers.

Air attacks continued throughout September with severe bomb and shell damage, including one shell crashing into the *Burlington Hotel*, one of the biggest properties in the town. Shells were also falling in the countryside just outside Dover.

Peter Bean, a 14-year-old boy at Dover County School (later Grammar School), was evacuated with his classmates to Ebbw Vale in Monmouthshire, but he returned to his home at Whitfield for the school holidays.

40   Burlington Hotel *hit*.

He remembers:

> I was able to witness much of the Battle of Britain in the sky above and that proved very
> exciting for a fourteen year old boy. My most vivid memory of that year was a near fatal
> incident for me. One sunny August morning I was on an East Kent double decker bus
> on my way to Dover. I was with another boy on the top deck. We were the only ones on
> that deck. Half way down Whitfield Hill, on our way to Dover, the bus stopped to pick
> up a couple who were walking to Dover. Before the bus restarted there was a flash and an
> almighty explosion which shattered some of the windows on the bus. We were extremely
> frightened, not knowing what had happened. We took little time in running home as fast
> as we could at top speed. We later discovered that a German shell, fired from France, was
> the cause. I think several others had fallen in the Kearsney area at that time. Luckily for
> us the shell landed in a field about fifty yards from the road. It killed two horses. If it had
> landed on the hard road I don't think I would be around today.

Norman Sutton's diary records:

> 11 September: Dover's worst day so far. Bombs and shells. The *Grand Hotel* badly damaged,
> the *Sailors Home* and the *Sussex Arms* wrecked. A time bomb fell on Folkestone Road.
> It got so bad at one stage the London evening papers arrived at Dover before the daily
> papers. London was being seriously attacked.

A group of Fleet Street and foreign journalists had made the *Grand Hotel* in Wellesley Road
their base and several of them escaped with their lives. Three or four were injured and had to
be helped out of the debris. American journalists were among those who flocked to Dover
expecting to write first-hand about the expected German invasion. One journalist provided
a long feature, entitled 'Front-line Town of Britain's Siege', for the *National Geographic*
magazine. He wrote:

> I stood on the cliffs, visiting a warden's post which is said to be the nearest one to the
> enemy. I found an old man, standing on the edge of the cliff, peering across the Strait at

41   Grand Hotel *hit.*

42   Grand Hotel *prior to demolition in 1947.*

enemy position. The French coast was plainly visible. The water was blue, the sky so clear and the whole scene was so peaceful that I found it hard to realize that at any moment a fleet of bombers might come diving down or a black messenger of death come hurtling across the sea. Lookouts have been placed at two of the highest points on the cliffs to give warning of gun flashes from the French coast. These lookouts keep logs and they are very methodical about entries such as 1312 hours – two gun flashes, 1313 hours – two shells. So is recorded for history the minute it takes for a shell to cross the Channel.

A bomb that brought down the *Sussex Arms* in Townwall Street led to an amazing rescue. A whimper was heard from the wreckage and a passing Royal Navy stoker crawled through the debris and brought out a little girl who was being sheltered in her mother's arms. The mother was dead.

Jack Hewitt MBE told of how he, too, was engaged in this rescue. His version of the drama was that around 26 bombs were dropped around the seafront, killing a total of 16 people: 'In the ruins of the pub a young mother saved her five month old baby, Jean Amos, throwing her body over the child's. I crawled into the ruins and helped to get the little girl out.'

Jack's story was told in the *Dover Express* and posed the question of where that little girl was now. As a result Mrs Jean Coleman (*née* Amos) contacted the newspaper, which arranged a reunion between her and Jack 40 years after that dramatic rescue.

43 *Clarence Street and Woolcomber Street damaged.*

In his autobiography, *Greetings, Dover!*, Jack claimed it was he who carried out the major part of the rescue, not the stoker who received the George Medal for his bravery. Jack claimed he was turned down for the award because he was a first-aid specialist who should not have been carrying out rescue work.

Dover businessman Ray Cook in his 1942 publication, *Shellfire Corner Carries on*, had this to say about his fellow townspeople: 'When the people of Dover hear bombs and bullets whistle, I believe they find something charming in the sound. They seem to thrive on war.'

Another, who somewhat over-egged the situation, was journalist Bernard Gray, who told the readers of the *Sunday Pictorial*:

I watched Nazi planes swoop down on Dover Streets. German Messerschmitts that had earlier shot down the barrage balloons, returned and dived down 'below the rooftops' in a furious onslaught on Britain's front line defence. Some of the German planes were so low you could see the pilots.

The Home Guard and the troops continued to guard and patrol Dover seafront, waiting for the invasion. While many soldiers were not supplied with guns (many had been lost at

44   *Liverpool Street.*

45   *Home Guard on patrol.*

Dunkirk) the Dover Home Guard was well supplied. They were looked upon as a suicide squad should the Germans invade. Norman Sutton, a Home Guard lieutenant, was issued with a Thompson sub-machine gun that he kept at home. Little did these patrolling Home Guardsmen know that about this time, 19 September, Hitler called off the invasion and began sending his soldiers eastwards, ready to fight Russia.

One of the most badly damaged properties in Dover was the museum, above the covered market in the Market Square. It was first damaged by a bomb on 21 October in 1940, when scores of exhibits including stuffed birds were scattered around the Square. It was bombed again on 23 March in 1942 and then hit by a shell on 4 October in 1943. Altogether the museum received serious damage on five occasions between 1940 and 1943.

Throughout October bombs and shells continued to fall on Dover with some near Connaught Barracks. Sirens, usually accompanied by bombing raids, sounded every day from the first day of the month until 23 October. In addition to the bombs there was regular shelling of the town. In one shelling incident a house was hit in Tower Street where four were killed.

Not far away from this, a shell hit Dover's wartime mortuary that was in use nearly every day throughout 1940. Ambulanceman Jack Hewitt, transporting a dead German pilot to the mortuary, was surprised to find one of his relations laid out there. Death came suddenly in Dover in 1940.

46   *Market Hall in the Market Square was hit five times between 1940 and 1943.*

47   *Christchurch School, Military Hill, hit.*

Walter Bates remembers:

It was the shelling that was the real evil. No warning was given until after the first shell arrived. Just instant death and injury from out of nowhere. The siren would howl and people took shelter but we never knew if the raid was just one shell or that another 20 would follow. As the years went by, with the shelling continuing, most of the town went about its business as usual. The people of Dover became hardened to this day-to-day existence.

Throughout all these raids were bands of school children whose parents had refused Home Office recommendations to send them to safety in Wales. They strolled through the town in groups, watching the troops and the air battles overhead. A small number of children who had been evacuated ran away from their South Wales foster parents to get home to their birth parents. Others came home on their parents' decision.

November was no better, with shelling almost daily and regular bombing raids. During the month the sirens wailed 141 times. Dover was getting used to the sound of sirens and many just went about their business. One bomb partly demolished the police station in Ladywell in the basement of which was the Civil Defence (CD) headquarters. Another bomb wrecked the Salvation Army centre, packed with servicemen. Many were killed.

48   *Dover Police Station hit.*

Dover's municipal sea bathing establishment on the seafront was hit and so badly damaged it closed for ever. The manager and manageress, Mr and Mrs Tom Huntley, were switched by their council employers to gas decontamination duties elsewhere in the town.

Councillors in October 1940 agreed to the removal from the Town Hall and the council chamber of valuable paintings and pictures to a place of safety. In the same month concern was expressed about the health of people sleeping in the town's deep air-raid shelters.

It was slightly quieter in the run-up to Christmas, but a parachute mine on 15 December caused massive damage. There was no enemy activity at Dover on Christmas Day, but there were four alerts on New Year's Eve, although the enemy decided to stay at home.

As a special concession, to provide entertainment for the hundreds of troops, Dover councillors allowed the Hippodrome to stage two shows on Christmas Day, on the condition none of the employees was forced to work.

Fleet Street journalist Reg Foster summed up Dover in 1940:

Dover could present an incongruous spectacle. Elderly men and women stroll up and down the seafront, quite oblivious that Jerry might come out of the sky at any moment and all hell would be let loose.

By the end of 1940, according to Norman Sutton's diary, Dover had had 570 siren alerts since the war started.

The cost of repairing bomb and shell-damaged highways in the town was so great that at the year's end the town council backed a Kent County Council demand to the government that the State should pay for the repair of the war-damaged roads. Dover was delighted to receive $1,000 from the Friends of Dover, England, in New Hampshire, USA, for the relief of townsfolk suffering distress as a result of enemy action.

During 1940, unknown to the people of Dover, as the threat of invasion grew, the military authorities and leading citizens of the town set up a Triumvirate that was to remain in force until October 1944 when Herbert Morrison at the Home Office considered it no longer necessary. This small group, meeting in secret, drew up plans to demolish scores of seafront properties and level the ground to provide lines of fire for the defenders against German invaders arriving at the port.

At first there were plans to set up a defence outpost at Buckland Bridge but later, with a shortage of troops, the two remaining centres of resistance were designated as Dover Castle and the Western Heights. A map was produced displaying a large sector of the town that the military required to be evacuated to Dover's deep shelters if there was an imminent threat of invasion. This would involve the movement of about four thousand people. Otherwise, all householders had to 'stay put' and not block roads. The military called for a 50 per cent reduction in Dover's population when it appeared an invasion was likely. Dover's town clerk estimated the town's population in December 1940 was down to 16,500 from 40,000 pre-war.

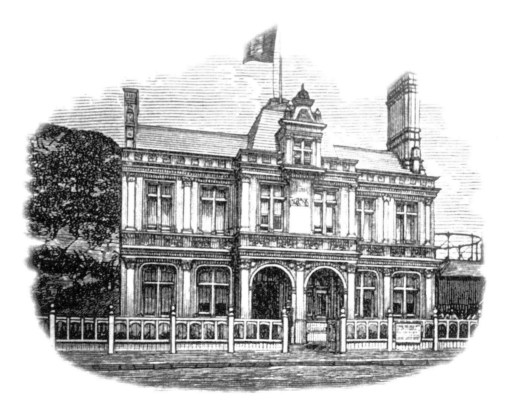

49 *Saltwater baths before damage.*

50   *Paintings in the Stone Hall, Dover Town Hall.*

'More are going out from the town than coming in,' the town clerk informed the military Garrison Commander. In reply a 'Top Secret' memo from Dover Castle to the Invasion Triumvirate read: 'The main object [of evacuation] is not the preservation of life but to facilitate military operations.'

At one stage the compulsory evacuation of Dover civilians was secretly considered. The combined military and civilian committee worked out they would be carried away from Dover in trainloads of 800 passengers. Before entraining, the enforced evacuees would congregate in the grounds of Dover College.

As the threat of invasion diminished there were still fears of a German commando-style raid on Dover and, as bomber attacks on England intensified, there were efforts by the government to get the Home Guard to help with Civil Defence duties, including fire-watching. There were counter moves to recruit CD workers for weapon training, but that did not go down well with the civilian authorities at Dover, who told the government it was impractical, especially as there was a shortage of CD volunteers.

Brigadier Geoffrey Harding, in a memo marked 'secret' from headquarters of 219 Infantry Brigade at Dover Castle, had different ideas. He wrote:

> All CD workers should be enrolled in a special local Home Guard battalion. They should continue with normal CD duties until I decide an attack against Dover is imminent. The men would then down their CD tools and take up their weapons to defend Dover to the last. Should an attack be beaten off they could revert to their CD duties.

Fortunately, there was no invasion!

1941

Settling down to Bombs and Shells

T HE YEAR 1941 started relatively quietly for Dover, although its citizens did not know that the threat of invasion was less likely. Thankfully the number of civilian casualties for the whole year was less than in 1940, but there remained plenty of danger, especially in the second half of the year. Dovorians were getting used to being bombed, machine-gunned by aircraft and shelled.

The town's three cinemas were usually packed with servicemen and women and with civilians, while the Hippodrome in Snargate Street did roaring business. Dances at the Town Hall were popular, especially with the soldiers and sailors looking for a girlfriend. There were even calls, resisted for months, to re-open the schools for the town's so-called 'dead end kids'.

Despite this air of ignoring the dangers there were plenty of bombing raids and shelling attacks – sometimes both at the same time. In January the German bombers tried to hit the Dover to Deal railway line above Astley Avenue. They failed to cut the line but bombs fell on either side, one at the back of Mayfield Avenue.

So far the Germans had not used firebombs on Dover, but on 16 January about a hundred of these incendiaries were scattered over a wide area of the town between the Pier District and Elms Vale. They did little damage thanks to swift action by firewatchers and Dover-based soldiers. One, however, remained undiscovered at the bonded warehouse on Custom House Quay down at the docks and caused damage.

The enemy's long-range guns that had remained silent for nearly three weeks fired at Dover at intervals for four hours on 18 January. The German news service announced their guns were firing at a convoy sailing along the coast near Dover.

Towards the end of the month more heavy gunfire could be heard but no shells were fired on Dover, so it appeared the enemy was aiming at Allied shipping in the Dover Strait.

It was reported by the British authorities around this time that shells had landed in the countryside at Barham. The German gunners were extending their range of fire.

51   *Hippodrome Theatre before damage.*

52   *Shells landing in Dover Harbour.*

53   Sussex Arms *before war damage.*

Virtually every day at Dover there were explosions heard on the other side of the Channel; the RAF was regularly bombing harbour installations, where invasion barges were still moored, and inland where 'slave workers' were engaged in constructing more long-range gun emplacements.

In early February a lone German bomber flew over the town, without being fired on, and dropped eight bombs that fell on military installations on the Western Heights and one on Victorian dwellings near the western docks.

There was an outburst of shelling during the second week of February during which some shells hit Ramsgate for the first time. The only casualties were six chickens. One shell landed near the railway line near Dover's famous *Lord Warden Hotel.*

February ended with bombs dropped on the last two days. Four bombs dropped in the Langdon area killed two soldiers and injured four others. Another bomb, near Dover seafront, completed the destruction of the *Sussex Arms*, badly damaged in the raid the previous September. Norman Sutton, in his diary, noted:

> The already seriously damaged area of Dover, around Townwall Street and St James' Street, seems to have a fatal attraction to the enemy. In this small area 118 houses have been totally destroyed and 172 seriously damaged.

All was fairly quiet during the first days of March, but on 9 March Germans bombed and shelled a convoy passing through the strait and the RAF was up attacking the enemy. The next day five bombs were dropped on Dover, including one on the seafront Granville Gardens which badly damaged the pavilion where, in peacetime, Dover people used to listen to the band and enjoy roller-skating. Other bombs dropped in the Granville Dock and an unexploded bomb was discovered in the basement of a house in Camden Crescent near the lodging house where Charles Dickens and his family had once stayed.

On the last day of the month there was more shelling. Six shells landed on Dover, causing serious injuries to Mrs Rosa Nicholls, 77, at her Bartholomew Street home and injuring five others. Mrs Nicholls died later. One of the other shells hit Flashman's furniture

54   *Popular Granville Gardens and the* Grand Hotel *pre-war.*

depository, where the belongings of evacuee families were stored, wrecking the building in Dieu Stone Lane at the back of St Mary's Church and tearing up tombstones. The site is now St Mary's parish centre.

Norman Sutton reported:

> For 117 consecutive days, from January 26th to May 22nd (almost four months) the sirens sounded every day, sometimes as often as ten times in 24 hours.
> The first week of April alone produced 42 alerts and on the 8th April Dover had the doubtful pleasure of announcing that its sirens had sounded for the 1,000th time.

Easter Sunday 1941 was celebrated by German pilots shooting down two barrage balloons during two attacks.

In April Dover obtained agreement with the Home Office to introduce a new siren warning system for shelling attacks. It was agreed that in the event of enemy shelling the siren would sound twice. When the shelling was over the 'All Clear' would be indicated with a single siren, but that could mean an air-raid warning was still in progress.

More shelling took place on 15 April but all the shells fell in the sea and it was suggested the enemy gunners were calibrating their guns.

In an early morning raid on 24 April a single German fighter bomber dropped a bomb that hit the iron foundry at Dover Engineering Works at Charlton Green, used by the RAF for the repair of barrage balloons. Two RAF men were injured.

There was more shelling that month and two soldiers sunbathing on a cliff ledge at the back of Trevanion Street (now the site of Dover sports centre) were killed. Six people were injured at various places in the town, four of them servicemen.

There was a long shelling warning on 29 April which lasted from 8.30 a.m. to 1.30 p.m., but none of the 77 shells hit the town. Most landed to the east of the town, some exploding in the air. German radio said their gunners were firing at military targets near Dover. It is probable the targets were the radar towers and installations at Swingate.

Cross-Channel shelling flared up again on 7 May when the enemy made one of the most violent attacks on the town. The British long-range gun 'Pooh' was brought into action for the first time, firing in harness with 'Winnie', the other British long-range gun. The Germans replied with three guns resulting in 11 shells landing on the town, causing three deaths with another 20 taken to hospital.

The deaths and most of the injuries were caused when a shell fell in the Market Square outside Westminster Bank. Those who died were Joseph Eeley, 54, Ethel May, 21, from Hougham, while Louie Pritchard, 18, from Clarendon Place died from her injuries in hospital.

There was anti-aircraft fire during the shelling raid and it transpired an enemy spotter plane was helping to direct the line of fire for the German gunners. Perhaps the spotters

55   *Caroline Place off Stembrook takes a beating.*

56   'Winnie' long-
range gun.

57   'Pooh' long-
range gun.

58   *Dover Town Hall (Maison Dieu).*

were trying to locate the huge British long-range guns in the Wanston area and the two railway guns that were taking part in the cross-Channel duels.

There were thousands of members of the armed forces based in Dover in 1941. In May that year an airman contacted the borough council, with a petition signed by 300 colleagues, asking the council to provide a roller skating venue in the town. He suggested the Connaught Hall in Dover's ancient Town Hall or the local dance centre in the Co-Op Hall in Maison Dieu Road (now demolished and the site prepared for housing). 'Sorry, not possible to arrange', the council replied.

One air attack was the machine gunning of a train that killed the driver, Mr P. Golding, and wounded his colleague. Folkestone was raided on 28 May and the mayor and mayoress, Mr and Mrs Gurr, were killed when a heavy bomb hit their home.

Earlier in the month the German aircraft attacked another convoy and two of the planes were shot down into the sea. The next day, 7 June, there were aircraft 'dog fights' over the town and over Whitfield, but no bombs were dropped.

There was an unusual incident on 10 June when a German pilot landed his machine, almost undamaged, near the second St Margaret's junction on the Dover-Deal road. One possibility was that he had lost his way and thought he was landing in France. The aircraft was a new-type ME 109F and the RAF specialists were delighted with their catch.

Mrs Phyllis Groombridge, now living at Eastry, was living at West Hougham in 1941 and she remembers an occasion when a German airman 'dropped in':

He had bailed out of his badly damaged aircraft and landed on our farm. My father, who was standing at the door of the house, heard something falling and ran to the bottom of the garden to find an injured German pilot. He called for assistance from Percy Atkins, a private in the Hougham Home Guard, who was assisted by other members of the Home Guard. They were able to release the German airman from his parachute and then carried him into the kitchen of the farmhouse. The police were called and he was taken to hospital. Of the 90 planes which came over our country that night 16 were known to be destroyed. At least 10 were brought down in the first attack.

Often there were duels between British and German gunners, especially when convoys were in the Strait. British bombers in mid-June attacked a 5,000-ton German tanker creeping along the French coast and sank it.

One of the worst wartime incidents in Dover did not result from bombs and shells. It caused the deaths in 1941 of 16 people, 20 were seriously injured and 23 wounded. It practically wiped out two entire families. It happened in the early morning, before dawn, on 12 June when a parachute mine floated gracefully down onto a row of houses in Randolph Road, working-class homes off what is now Coombe Valley Road. The crew of the low-flying German plane that dropped the massive bomb, attached to a parachute, was probably aiming at the gas works 100 yards away. There was a terrific explosion

59   *Captured German pilot at Hougham.*

60   *Randolph Road decimated.*

and a blinding flash seen over a wide area of the town that woke up many people. The parachute mine had landed in the garden of homes near the bottom of the road, bringing down virtually all the houses in the street. Home Guardsmen on duty at the gas works were among the first on the scene and, with the help of soldiers, began digging out the dead and injured.

Those who were killed were Mr and Mrs John Willis, their sons Horace and Brian, their 16-year-old daughter, Vera, and a married daughter, Hilda Mills (six out of the seven in the family); Mr and Mrs Fred Moore and their two-month-old son, Frederick, and Minyon Elsie (aged four); Mr and Mrs Frederick Cock; Doris Smith (aged three); and Charlie Talbot whose wife Minnie died in Maidstone hospital three weeks later from her injuries. The damage was so bad that more than forty houses in Randolph Road and Union Road (as it was then called) had to be demolished. Barry Fincham remembers that night well. He recalls:

> An air-raid warning was sounded but no enemy planes were heard. So we went back to bed. Then there was a huge explosion some time later and the sky was seen to be glowing over the Union Road area but no planes could be heard. Next morning I tried to see what had happened but was not able to get very far up Union Road as the pavements were ankle deep in debris. Then I saw that Randolph Road, where my grandparents lived, was obliterated. Very little was found of my grandfather and my grandmother died a few weeks later from her injuries. I felt sick.

61   War effort: keeping chickens.

62   War effort: buy a war weapon.

The gas works and gasometer were severely damaged but the employees worked hard and gas supplies were back on stream within five hours.

With horrendous losses of merchant ships in the Atlantic and elsewhere, there was a great danger that the British would starve to death as the amount of imported food diminished. In Dover there was a quick response to government appeals to 'Dig for Victory' as townsfolk began to grow more food on their allotments. Some dug up front gardens, even on the seafront, where chicken coops were also set up. As the war continued there were also official calls for citizens to save and invest money in aircraft, ships and tanks. Thousands of pounds were saved in this way in Dover.

Prime Minister Winston Churchill visited the Dover area on 20 June and ordered increased defences to counter any German small-unit landings, as British Commandoes were occasionally doing along the French coast.

He inspected the network of pipes that would shoot burning oil onto the sea if the enemy attempted a landing. Much of the pipe work had been manufactured in Dover Harbour Board's workshops in Cambridge Road near the seafront – properties now converted to provide shopping facilities at De Bradlie Wharf.

Two days after Churchill's visit the Germans made the fatal mistake of launching their attack on Russia.

In the early days of July there were three occasions when German guns and aircraft attacked British convoys off Dover. These attacks were followed up with shelling of the St Margaret's area where British long-range guns were based. On 25 July there was another attack on a British convoy when one of the enemy shells landed on Barwick's builders yard in Market Street (just off the Market Square) causing considerable damage but no injuries. The final shelling of the

63 *Winston Churchill looking out to sea from Castle observation post.*

64   *Churchill inspecting the coastal guns.*

month came on 30 July when it was estimated that the German long-range guns had fired about a total of 3,500 rounds. Norman Sutton's diary comments:

> Many of these shells had been fired at shipping and therefore had fallen in the sea. But they had been responsible for about half the 80-odd civilians killed in the town.
>   At this stage 436 homes in the town had been badly damaged. More than 100 families had lost their homes from war damage.

65   *Norman Sutton,*
reporter and weather man.

Apart from his editor, John Bavington Jones, Norman Sutton was the only working journalist in Dover throughout the war. When war was declared in 1939 the British censors banned details of weather conditions in the United Kingdom because such information would help the enemy decide when to make air attacks. Even in 1940 the *Dover Express*, looking back over the previous 12 months, explained it was prevented from detailing much about the year's weather.

A dramatic change came in 1941 when someone in Whitehall or in Parliament realised this was ineffective. The Germans were dug in on the French coast and could easily see what the weather was like in the Dover Strait. So permission was given by the authorities for newspapers to report on the day's weather conditions at Dover.

Fleet Street editors began contacting Norman Sutton asking him to do the daily job of providing the weather reports. He agreed, went out and bought a minimum and maximum outdoor thermometer while the GPO swiftly installed a telephone at his Stanhope Road home, despite it being almost impossible for civilians to get a phone. So each day, sometimes twice a day, Home Guard Lieutenant Norman Sutton rang the weather conditions to a number of Fleet Street newspapers. This was on top of working long hours at the *Dover Express* office in Snargate Street.

One day he used the public box in Maison Dieu Road to phone his weather report. A passing regular army officer heard him, waited until he finished and then 'arrested' him as a suspected spy. He marched Mr Sutton at revolver point to the police station in Ladywell where he was very well known for his daily calls. The officer sheepishly apologised and went on his way.

When Norman died, long after the war ended, his obituary in *The Times* conceded that he probably had more wartime front page items in national newspapers than any other reporter.

66   *Norman Sutton leads Home Guard parade.*

There was not much serious crime in Dover during the war years although the authorities stuck up notices on walls warning that the penalty for looting from war-damaged property was death or life imprisonment. There was very little looting! One crime that was the talk of the town in 1941 was the murder, with an axe, of a Dover cinema manager whose body was dumped in the basement. After an investigation an 18-year-old cinema operator was charged, convicted and sentenced to be hanged. More than 3,000 people signed a petition seeking a reprieve and the Home Secretary, the day before the teenager was due to be executed, relented and imposed a sentence of penal servitude for life.

On 6 August there was more shelling of the town with hits in the Union Road and Magdala Road area. Other shells were at Old Park and at the Camber at the Eastern Docks (now built over) where a civilian dockyard worker was seriously injured. Whitfield received two shells on 17 August with another near the Duke of York's School from where the boys had been evacuated. A lone plane attacked with six bombs, one of which damaged the workshops in Cambridge Road and another fell near the Wellington Dock slipway (now covered over for car parking).

In September 1941 the Luftwaffe tried a new weapon, chaining three high-explosive bombs together. One fell on the slopes above St James' cemetery, narrowly missing the graves of servicemen who had died during the Dunkirk evacuation.

On 7 September a lone bomber escaped detection and, with no attack expected, dropped a stick of bombs, one of which hit the already badly damaged *Burlington Hotel* near the seafront. Here again the bombs might have been chained together. Of the five people still living in this once smart hotel, three were killed. They were William Horne, the caretaker Joseph Turner and his wife Rosa.

67   *Duke of York's Royal Military School.*

A well-known Dover butcher and one time councillor Albert Decort had a remarkable escape. He recalled:

> I was in the bathroom, seated on the toilet, when the bomb crashed into the hotel. The floor gave way, I grabbed the first thing I could and was left hanging on the lavatory cistern.

The *Burlington Hotel* was now so badly damaged it had to be demolished, after which the army did using explosives.

Dover's 1,500th alert was sounded on 15 September and the next day there was shelling and bombing of the town. On that night the Germans brought into use a very strong searchlight which they shone across the Strait, apparently to illuminate the sea for convoys or for attacking Allied MTBs that were harassing German shipping.

One of the most damaging bomb attacks on Dover came on 17 September when the dropping of only five bombs resulted in the death of three people as well as injuring five seriously. A single enemy plane crossed the Channel and was over Dover soon after 8 p.m. and, diving from the east, released its bombs apparently with Chitty's Mill in the Charlton Green area as its target.

One bomb fell at the back of the *Red Lion* public house and the others were strung out over Granville Street and Bartholomew Street, causing the destruction of 10 houses. Found dead under the debris were Edward Dive, 58, his 14-year-old son Fred, who had narrowly escaped the parachute mine in Randolph Road three months earlier, and John Hatton, sixty-nine. The seriously injured included: Mrs Dive, Mrs Hatton, Albert Humphreys, 63, Ernest Horton, 40, and Harry Wilson, forty.

October brought three bombing attacks causing casualties in each. The first was during brilliant moonlight when nine or ten bombs were dropped in a string from Military Hill, close to a military establishment, to the sea. Night watchman Frederick Bexall, 62, of Beaufoy Terrace was killed. One bomb overturned an army lorry and two soldiers were injured. It is believed the targets were groups of six-inch guns on the cliffs at the Western Heights.

One of the worst dive-bomb attacks on Dover came over five hours on the night of 2 October. This attack killed nine civilians and five servicemen. A total of 80 people were injured. Strangely, that night there was a switch-over of anti-aircraft gun crews and the dive-bombing came during the hours before the replacement crews had arrived on station. The two sets of crews were passing each other on the Canterbury road when the dive-bombers first arrived. This, quite naturally, led to suspicions among some Dovorians that a spy had tipped off the Germans.

Much damage was caused when a bomb exploded in the roadway near the *Red Cow* public house (since demolished; the site is near the Folkestone Road-York Street roundabout).

But the worst incident was when four bombs smashed into Dour Street, wrecking many homes that were eventually demolished and where, post-war, flats were built on the

site. One of the residents of Dour Street
was William Barton, a police officer based
in the nearby police station. He hurried
home to 36 Dour Street to find his home
destroyed. His daughter, Mrs Rosemary
Wells, of London Road, Dover, recalls that
he feared the worst for his wife and daughter,
but after a search found them uninjured in a
garden air-raid shelter, although it had been
squashed to a third of its size.

In all about forty bombs were dropped
in three waves of attacks, most of which fell
between Folkestone Road and the seafront,
in the Pier District and some in the sea.
Norman Sutton records:

> In addition to the houses destroyed about
> 1,800 homes and other property had to
> receive first aid repairs, from broken
> windows upwards.

Among those killed that night were William
Stacey, 66, of the Ropewalk, Alfred Court,
50, of Limekiln Street and Albert Greer, 69,
of Snargate Street.

During one phase of the attack a soldier,
Gunner Carpenter, saved the life of Doreen

68   *Priory Road hit.*

Hart of Clarendon Street who had been attending a concert in the Wesley Hall in Folkestone
Road. He heard the bomb coming and threw Doreen to the ground and covered her with
his body. He was so seriously injured that he had to have a leg amputated. Wesley Hall,
damaged in the First World War and rebuilt, was very badly damaged. After repairs a plaque
on the wall told of the hall's battered history.

Other deaths that night included retired innkeeper James Tapsell, 68, of Dour Street
and his wife Annie, 68, who were buried in the wreckage of their home. Next-door
neighbour Patrick Carberry, 83, was fatally injured by falling masonry. Another Dour
Street resident who lost his life was Frank Field, sixty-nine. Mrs Mary Dyer of Military
Hill and a baker, Mr Dobson, both died in hospital from their injuries along with a
number of servicemen. One was George Bowling, 27, of Priory Hill who was home on
leave from the Royal Navy.

Over the next 10 days there were three occasions when the long-range guns on the French
coast fired at shipping off Dover but no shells fell in the town.

At the time Phyllis Groombridge, then aged 14, was working for her farmer father as a shepherdess and she saw plenty of action:

I used to tend the sheep in fields on the cliffs between Dover and Capel, overlooking what is now Samphire Hoe. I used to watch the convoys passing by in the Channel, often guarded by Spitfires and Hurricanes. This was the time when there were often dog fights and on one occasion I got under a corn shelter for protection and could hear bullets and shrapnel hitting the roof. Funnily enough I used to love those days. When on the cliffs, depending on weather conditions, I would sometimes be able to see the flashes when the Germans fired shells from the French coast.

On 1 October a launch out of Dover picked up four Belgian men and a woman, drifting in a small boat in a minefield. They had fled at night from Belgium and had drifted for two days.

Later in October British fighters intercepted a group of enemy bombers which, in a hurry to get rid of their bombs, dropped them on Dover. Two

people, Mr and Mrs Sydney Davis, were killed in Stanhope Road and five seriously injured. On that night scores of incendiary bombs were dropped, about seventy at Hougham, and caused a number of small fires.

Two days later, while a convoy was being shelled in the Strait, there was thunder and lightning that brought down four barrage balloons in flames.

69 *Wesley Methodist Church, Folkestone Road, hit again.*

It was during October that six schools re-opened for the first time in 18 months. This was against the wishes of the education authority at Dover, who feared the opening would attract more evacuees to return home – which it did.

On the afternoon of Saturday 1 November, servicemen were playing football on one of the grounds at Dover Grammar School for Boys at Astor Avenue. A shell fell close by, killing a soldier and a sailor. Also killed was William Norley, 52, who was working on his allotment nearby.

That was the only shelling raid in November but there were three bombing attacks. In the first, on 7 November, no one was killed but nine people were injured on the Castle estate. The following evening five bombs were dropped in the Ropewalk area, killing Arthur Skelton, 39, who was standing at his back door in King Lear Way. Albert Kenton, 80, was buried under the debris of a house and died in hospital nine days later.

During the month there were sea battles off the French coast when Dover- and Ramsgate-based MTBs attacked German shipping. German radio claimed to have destroyed one of the MTBs.

December saw the Japanese attack on Pearl Harbour that brought America into the war, but in Dover it was a relatively quiet month. In that month Victoria Wellard, aged 12, was in South Wales when her mother visited her. A decision was made that Victoria should return to her home in Dover's Beach Street. Victoria (now Mrs Walter of Bilting, Ashford) recalls:

> In those days Beach Street, not far from Shakespeare Beach and the *Lord Warden Hotel*, was the front line town's front line street. When we got back to Dover I had to be taken to the police station to get a certificate to show that I lived in the security area near the docks. We slept nearly every night in the caves situated at the back of the Oil Mills (now the site of a petrol filling station) in Limelkiln Street. We used to go there every evening about six o'clock and return home next morning. For a while I attended the Pier infant school because, I think, that was the only one open.
>
> Then I started work at a shop called Kays Ways Pays in Cannon Street, opposite St Mary's Church, which traded in groceries. One day I went to work and the shop was wrecked and so it closed down. A shell had crashed through the front of the shop. So then I went to work at the Co-Op head office where, during raids, we went down in the basement cellar. There were some hectic days that continued into the nights, so on those occasions, we remained in the basement. On one occasion we came out of the basement at three in the morning so I then walked down to Limekiln Street to join the others in the Oil Mill caves. I think that was the night when there was a big bomb in the Market Square.

Nothing serious happened in December until 10 days before Christmas when the enemy shelled shipping in the Channel, with 20 shells falling on Dover. One fell in the middle of the road at Stanhope Road, damaging the façades of several houses and killing a soldier who was billeted there.

The following evening enemy aircraft dropped flares over the town and then dropped 10 high-explosive bombs and about one hundred and fifty firebombs. Only two people were

70   *Oil Mill Caves party.*

71   *Cannon Street damage.*

slightly hurt. Two of the firebombs landed on the roof of the GPO (the site occupied until recently by the former Woolworths) but were quickly dealt with by postmen.

On Christmas Eve a few shells from enemy guns were fired at a convoy and the sirens were sounded in Dover. On Christmas Day bombs were dropped in the countryside outside Dover. That proved to be the last enemy action of 1941.

1942

Invasion Threat

HEAVY SNOW FELL in January 1942, but this did not prevent air and shelling activity on the south-east coast. Norman Sutton observed that the enemy gunners appeared to be using a different type of shell when attacking Dover. The shells did not explode on impact but exploded two or three minutes after arrival. This was confirmed when one shell fell in the back garden of a house in Maison Dieu Road, near Pencester Gardens, causing a larger crater than normal.

Dover was in the world's headlines again in February 1942 when, on a gloomy misty day, the German battleships *Gneisenau* and *Scharnhorst* with the heavy cruiser *Prinz Eugen* slipped through the Strait. They had been bottled up by the Royal Navy in the captured French port of Brest and were making a dash for homeland ports. In his war diary Norman Sutton commented that with such bad weather Dovorians would normally expect a relatively peaceful day.

Lack of action on intelligence by the British gave no central warning of the enemy warships' movements until it was too late for effective Royal Navy action. The Fleet Air Arm attacked, however, suffering heavy losses, while the long-range guns at St Margaret's Bay and Wanston opened up with a terrific barrage. Small coastal craft were sent out from Dover and carried out torpedo attacks but ran into stiff opposition from the German craft defending their battleships.

The first attack on the German warships was made soon after midday on 12 February by all the available MTBs from Dover, but there were only five that were serviceable. The MTBs roared out of the harbour five minutes before midday and sighted the enemy half an hour later between Calais and Gravelines. The Germans, determined on Hitler's orders to get the battleships to a home port, put up a huge screen of escorting torpedo boats and S-boats and prevented the Dover MTBs getting closer than 4,000 yards. Messersschmitts made sure

72 *Wanston long-range gun.*

they got no closer. Shortly after, six Swordfish of the Fleet Air Arm joined in the mêlée but were shot down and the Dover MTBs were kept busy picking up the aircraft survivors.

When the British long-range guns opened up there was a swift reply from the German guns on the French coast and a terrific duel ensued. The German fleet made it through the English Channel to different ports, leading to some homeland criticism about the heavy losses suffered by the Fleet Air Arm.

Women's Auxiliary Air Force (WAAF) staff, based at Abbots Cliff House on the clifftop at Capel, say they gave early warnings about large-scale enemy movements in the Channel that day but allege no heed was taken by the British command. The WAAF staff, usually German linguists, kept a 24-hour radio listening watch and information picked up was sent to the Enigma codebreakers at Bletchley Park.

March opened with another shelling of a British convoy passing through the Strait and later that day Dovorians heard loud explosions in the Channel. This was the result of Dover-based MTBs attacking a German convoy off the French coast when one enemy tanker was torpedoed and sunk. Two nights later there were more heavy explosions in a battle between German minesweepers and Allied MTBs, including those based at Dover and manned by Norwegians. Guns on both sides of the Channel were in action on 9 March when Allied and German light coastal craft clashed off the French coast between Calais and Boulogne.

The reduced population of Dover became used to seeing some strange characters passing through the town. Sometimes they were German prisoners, occasionally shot-down pilots, but more often a commando unit just back from 'raiding' the French coast, to destroy installations or to capture an unsuspecting German soldier. Richard Spear, now living in

British Columbia, recalls one occasion when a bunch of Allied soldiers drifted through the town centre:

> I was staying with my aunt at the popular *Queen's Head* public house [Boots the Chemists is now situated on the site] when we saw these soldiers who were not dressed in normal military uniforms. They wore no caps but woollen hats. Some of them spoke in a strange language. Later I discovered they were troops from the French part of Canada.
>
> On another occasion, so I was told by my aunt Mrs Pritchard, a senior officer came into the bar and gave her several pounds and told her to use it for any of his unit who came in for a drink. It was Lord Lovat who, with his commando, had just returned from a raid on the French coast.

On 22-3 March 1942 this commando unit, led by Major Lord Lovat, set off from Dover in an MTB and landed on the French coast west of Boulogne to test the enemy's defences. On his return to Dover he was questioned by Admiral Bertram Ramsay, commanding officer at Dover, on a mist-shrouded quayside.

73   *A captured German minelayer in Dover Harbour.*

One of Dover's worst air raids came on a moonlit evening on 23 March, after almost a week without a siren, when 20 heavy calibre bombs were dropped by dive bombers, killing 16 people and injuring seven others. Most of the loss of life was caused when a bomb penetrated an air-raid shelter in the East Kent garage in St James' Street, killing most of those inside. During the same raid, the East Kent's office in the Market Square was also hit, killing more members of the bus company's staff.

Another serious incident during the raid was when a bomb struck one end of the Conservative Party's unofficial headquarters at the Carlton Club in the Market Square, killing four well-known townsfolk including a town councillor. A soldier outside the club was killed by falling masonry.

The British military had created 'dummy' long-range guns some safe distance from the actual guns and the area around these false guns was pitted with bomb craters after the attack. The real guns escaped.

Allan Edgington, home on holiday from the grammar school at Ebbw Vale, remembers Easter 1942 very well:

> I remember the Messerschmitts came over and shot down nearly all the barrage balloons. Next night was a full moon, just right for a raid. My father, serving in the Home Guard, was out on duty and my mother and I decided to get under the stairs for protection. Our shelter, in Knight's Way, was at the end of a long garden and it was a cold night. As we huddled under the stairs we could hear the fighter-bombers diving down on the town, then the whistle of the bombs. The first one exploded on the railway line where it passes between Buckland Mill and Hillside Road. The second landed on the hillside, near a small wood, not far from Friars Way where it exploded. You could still the see the scar it left on the hillside, even in 1966.

74 *East Kent bus garage hit.*

In April, Dover Borough Council again asked the government to insist upon the compulsory evacuation of all children of school age from Dover, but in October part-time elementary education restarted in Dover and this resulted in an increase in the number of evacuated children 'drifting back' to the town. One of those was John J. Smith. He explained why:

75   *St James' Street, March 1942.*

76   *Carlton Club, Market Square.*

I received a letter from home saying our house in Stembrook had been destroyed by an enemy shell. Luckily my mum and dad were OK. When the shell fell mum was out shopping and dad was at work at Tilmanstone Colliery. Because he worked at the colliery, after the shell destroyed our house he was allocated a pit house some seven miles outside Dover in the village of Elvington. My parents came to South Wales to pick me up and take me to our new abode which had three bedrooms and was in the country.

The Board of Education in 1942 estimated there were a thousand children taking part in 'half time' education in Dover but, because that was not compulsory, attendance was irregular, while a large number were not going to school at all. The Board called on the local education authority to make all children in Dover go to school even if only for half a day.

A number of evacuated children returned home from the safety of Wales to Dover for the school holidays. Head teachers at evacuated schools, not in favour of this, pointed out the danger of doing so. Allan Edgington, who was aged about eleven at the time, was one of those who returned to Dover to celebrate Christmas in 1941. Others joined the flood of those going home for the holidays not long afterwards.

The Ministry of Health tried to persuade the local education authority to open the schools full time but Dover refused, pointing out that it would result in even more youngsters returning to Dover. Instead, the education authority at Dover, worried about the safety of the children, requested that evacuation be made compulsory, but

77   *Children of St Martin's School return.*

78   *Dover evacuees' reunion, 1994.*

in June that year the Ministry refused that idea and insisted evacuation should remain voluntary. The education authority in Dover, however, bowed to Whitehall pressure and nine schools were opened for compulsory education, which did attract more children to return home. By November 1942, according to official education figures, there were 1,687 boys and girls at schools in Dover with only 574 remaining in reception areas in South Wales.

A year later, again according to official statistics, there were only 340 Dover elementary school children in South Wales and 2,156 attending schools in Dover. Rolls at the two Dover grammar schools (formerly county schools) slimmed down slightly with the boys at Ebbw Vale and the girls at Caerleon.

Towards the end of 1944 parents, especially a vocal group in Deal, were demanding that the remaining evacuees should be brought home. At first this was refused but eventually the education authorities relented.

The great day for the two grammar schools came just before Christmas 1944 when a special train carried the boys and girls back to a badly battered Dover. But problems were not over. The girls could return to their school in Frith Road but the boys' school at Astor Avenue was still occupied by the WRNS so Dover Grammar School boys, under headmaster

79   *Dover County School for Boys.*

John C. Booth, were taught for several months in separate buildings: the former technical college in Ladywell, the School of Art in Maison Dieu Road and Hillersdon House in Godwyne Road.

Eventually the WRNS moved out of the boys' grammar school building and moved into other accommodation. During the war they had occupied parts of the requisitioned *Lord Warden Hotel* (named HMS *Wasp*) and property at Dover College. HMS *Wasp* was also the administrative centre for the MTBs based at Dover. HMS *Lynx* was another Royal Navy base at Dover.

The British government was still concerned about the possibility of a German invasion and in June 1942 the Home Office contacted Dover town council recommending what should be done to prepare for such an eventuality. The town clerk told the council's general purposes committee that in the event of an invasion a triumvirate would take control of the town, consisting of the mayor, the commanding officer of the Dover garrison and the chief officer of police. They would carry out the duties of an 'Invasion Committee'. In a further move that summer George Plater, assistant mains engineer with the local electricity undertaking, was appointed chief security officer tasked to prevent sabotage of vital equipment in the event of an invasion.

Through the months of spring and summer there were constant duels between the British and German gunners, often when a convoy was passing through the Strait.

John J. Smith, whose family had moved out of Dover to Elvington, had a narrow escape. He recalls:

A few of us, all boys, used to take a bus into Dover to go to the pictures. On one occasion we had been to the Plaza cinema in the high street and we had to walk through the town to near Buckland Bridge to catch the bus home. The buses never came right into Dover for safety reasons. As we got to the bottom of Tower Hamlets Road, not far from the Plaza, there was an almighty bang. A German shell had landed right outside the cinema that we had just left. We were lucky. It might have been us who were killed.

August passed without a casualty in Dover from either bombing or shelling, but both took their toll in September.

On 4 September three shells were fired at the dock area. One hit the former Dunkirk ferry dock where MTBs were often concealed, injuring three naval ratings. At lunchtime on 5 September, two 500-kilo and two 250-kilo bombs were dropped by high-flying aircraft. One hit Albert Road, demolishing two houses and killing two women. As a result of the air raid 15 people were also injured, 10 being taken to hospital.

The following day saw another air raid with more 500-kilo bombs dropped. The property most damaged was the synagogue, off Northampton Street. In their news service the German radio said they had hit dock installations.

Later the same day seven shells out of 26 fired fell on the town, killing one man, serving in the Home Guard, at Pioneer Road and seriously injuring seven others. One of those injured was Albert Decort, who had escaped death when the *Burlington Hotel* was hit. He was cycling to his butchery business from Alkham where he had gone to live after his hotel flat was destroyed.

Dover Borough Council brought into use in September loudspeakers erected at various points in the town centre to warn of enemy action in an attempt to save lives, especially servicemen and women who had orders to take cover when warnings were broadcast.

Mrs Audrey Wood, a little girl during the war, remembers one incident during shelling:

Our family lived above my father's shop, Wright's shoe shop, opposite the Town Hall, and when a raid warning was given we used to run across the main street into the old police station under the

80   *Members of the WRNS relaxing in Dover.*

Town Hall and take shelter in one. There were many explosions to be heard, but on one occasion there was a terrific explosion and a woman came into the shelter to tell my mother that all her best china had been smashed and was all over the street. When we emerged from the shelter we saw the broken china, but it was from the china-constructed nameplate on the façade of my father's shop that had been shattered by shrapnel.

Two visitors to the town on 23 September were Prime Minister Winston Churchill and South African leader Field Marshal Smuts, who inspected military and naval units as well as meeting civilians.

There were a few red faces on this visit. The commanding officer of the gunners

81   *Winston Churchill and General Smuts in Dover.*

82   *Churchill at Castle gun emplacement.*

83   *A shell-damaged Dover home.*

wanted to show off to his visitors a new weapon designed to beat the attacking German bombers and fighters. It was a kind of 'aerial minefield' that was fired over the harbour in front of the attackers. The idea was the Luftwaffe pilots would fly into the minefield which would explode and bring down the aircraft. But something went wrong and the unexploded anti-aircraft mines floated shorewards and part fell on the office roof of the local newspaper, the *Dover Express*, in Snargate Street. It took some time to clear the explosives from the roof. Churchill was not amused.

October was relatively quiet except for Monday 5 October when 14 shells fell on the town, killing four people and injuring another 14 people. One shell fell in Adrian Street where the four were killed. Another shell fell on the Dover to Deal railway line but this was soon repaired. One fell in Norman Street, wrecking a house and bringing the debris down on Dover's town sergeant, John Chapman, who had to be dug out. During the following week there were 28 siren alerts, but no air raids developed.

November brought more shelling on three occasions but there were no casualties in the town; however, during one shelling attack 11 anti-aircraft gunners were killed near St Margaret's.

There were only two shelling alerts in December, once again after the British guns near St Margaret's opened fire. Several of the returning shells from France were airbursts. An Eythorne taxi driver was killed in Folkestone Road and another shell falling at the back of Victoria Street killed Doris Moore, aged 16.

84   *Land Army girls.*

85   *Long-range gun at Lydden.*

On 15 December the bodies of a number of German naval men, picked up in the Channel, were landed at Dover and taken to the town mortuary. Three other Germans were rescued from a raft by Sergeant Pilot Tom Fletcher of the Air-Sea Rescue Service at Dover, who taxied his seaplane through three minefields to pick up the exhausted men. He then, with his prisoners, was guided back into Dover harbour by a searchlight provided by the Dover Harbour Board tug *Lady Brassey*. The enemy trio, suffering from exposure, were taken to Buckland Hospital and later Fletcher was awarded the Distinguished Flying Medal for his bravery.

While the borough of Dover was being bombarded, the rural area around the town was also receiving its fair share of bombs and shells. For its size the parish of St Margaret's-at-Cliffe, within the boundaries of which the British long-range guns were situated, received even greater punishment than the town.

Official figures released at the end of the war for Dover Rural Council's area showed that in the villages only five civilians were killed, 10 seriously injured and another eight slightly injured. That was remarkably light considering that 686 shells exploded on the ground and many more were fired to burst in the air. In addition, 389 high-explosive bombs and more than 2,300 fire bombs were dropped in the rural area.

Because most of the flying bombs were routed to the west of Dover, several blew up in the area around Capel-le-Ferne. A total of 21 flying bombs landed in the Dover rural area while others, hit by anti-aircraft fire, blew up in the air over the villages.

Figures published at the end of the war showed that 36 homes were wrecked by enemy action, 141 severely damaged and just under two thousand received slight damage.

While shells were being fired from the French coast, farm workers including Land Army girls continued to till the fields. This work continued on farmland within easy sight of the British guns at Wanston and St Margaret's, where it was accepted that firing by them would get a rapid response by the German gunners on the other side of the Strait.

Former Land Army worker Pat Solley told the *Dover Express* that her instructions from the Ministry of Defence, in the event of a German invasion, were: 'Put on your tin hat, keep milking the cows and dismantle the tractors so they can't be used by the enemy.'

The British cross-Channel guns ringed St Margaret's Bay with the 14-inch guns named Winnie and Pooh to the east and west and more large guns at South Foreland, Fan Bay, and Wanston. These long-range guns were backed up by more guns that ran to their firing positions on railway lines and when not in use were hidden away in railway tunnels at Shepherdswell and Guston. Railway arches were reinforced to carry the weight of the guns and their support wagons. Some of the bridge-supporting superstructure work remains in place today.

86   *Gladiator 13½-inch railway-mounted gun at St Margaret's.*

87   *'Jane' long-range gun at St Margaret's.*

88   *Eighteen-inch railway-mounted Howitzer.*

1943

Dover Ablaze

THERE WERE DEFINITE signs that the war was swinging in favour of the Allies in 1943 and with victories in North Africa and on the Russian front the enemy was often too busy to attack Dover. It proved to be a relatively quiet year but the German guns continued to shell the town and there were still a number of air raids.

In January the anti-aircraft guns were often in action as German planes flew over the town on their way to carry out raids on London, seen as reprisals for Allied bombing raids on German cities. One night, on 18 January, the enemy planes, flying high, encircled the town but the heavy fire from Dover gun emplacements drove them off, although not before containers of incendiaries were dropped. They caused fires on the Clarendon estate where four houses were seriously damaged and others slightly damaged. The firebomb containers were found near the Priory Station and at Northbourne Avenue.

Walter Bates, living with his family at 13 Percival Terrace, remembers that night vividly. His home was fire bombed:

> My dad realised it was going to be a bad raid and the family ran hell for leather along the back alley. We arrived safely in the caves and I remember looking back towards the Clarendon estate. The hills were a mass of flame while there was tremendous thumping of bombs dropping and the terrific noise of the anti-aircraft barrage. It was like the end of the world. When, much later, when we came out of the shelter, we were told a house in Percival Terrace was in flames. It proved to be our home at 13 Percival Terrace.
>
> We later discovered that a basket bomb, full of incendiaries, had crashed through the roof onto my parents' bed and exploded. Mum and dad were devastated. We now had no home, no clothes, no food. All gone.

Two high-explosive bombs were also dropped but they failed to explode. One was at River where RAF men had a lucky escape. The unexploded bomb went clean through the veranda of Brooklands, at the junction of Common Lane and Lower Road, just missing the airmen who almost fell into the hole created. Because the bomb had failed to explode 50 people were evacuated from their homes and accommodated in River Village Hall. It was weeks before the bombs could be made safe, partly because one had fallen near the bank of the River Dour and had penetrated deep into the wet soil.

On the evening of 8 February enemy aircraft were over Dover harbour trying to lay mines near the entrance to the port. Before dawn the next day the Germans began shelling Dover in the first time for two months. It was the British long-range guns that began the firing and that set off the German guns in retaliation. Their shells straddled the St Margaret's area, where our guns were situated, resulting in the death of a soldier and a civilian from Folkestone working in the Navy, Army, Air Force Institute (NAAFI) at Fan Bay. These were the first enemy action fatalities of the year on land.

There was more shelling of Dover in March with some damage caused but no deaths. Norman Sutton in his war diary commented:

> March passed without notable incidents in the town. It would scarcely be correct to describe it as a quiet month for the siren sounded almost every day, sometimes four or five times a day. By the end of the month the Dover sirens had been heard 2,275 times.

Out in the Channel, off Dover, there was plenty of action, with MTBs attacking enemy shipping and minesweepers carrying out the dangerous task of clearing mines. Dover-based air-sea rescue craft were also busy dashing to sea to pick up pilots and crew of Allied aircraft that had ditched in the Channel on their way home from enemy-occupied lands. The bodies of enemy pilots were also recovered.

One British airman whose body was washed up between Dover and Folkestone was Flight-Sergeant Middleton, whose Stirling aircraft just failed to make it to Kent after a raid on the Fiat Works in Turin. On his orders five of the crew baled out, but two remained with him and died when the aircraft plunged into the sea. Middleton was posthumously awarded the Victoria Cross.

Walter Nicholl recalls one amusing incident:

> My brother Peter was on a reconnaissance flight in a Mosquito over the Channel when one of his engines packed up. He flew back towards the coast hoping to get to Manston, but then the second engine failed and he came down around Stelling Minnis. He decided to call on his mother who asked if he had been given a spot of leave. He explained he was not on leave but had crashed not that far away.

April brought more cross-Channel duels between the heavy guns on both sides of the Strait which often resulted in enemy shells crashing down on Dover. One shell landed at the back of The Paddock, off Maison Dieu Road, and a property was so badly damaged it had to be pulled down. A woman in the adjoining house escaped with slight injuries. Another shell fell alongside St James' churchyard off Woolcomber Street, causing casualties among a number of soldiers who were exercising. Two soldiers on a gun site in Union Road were killed when enemy aircraft dropped bombs on 17 April. The German gunners began firing at irregular intervals into the town and, it was believed, this was to anger the civilian

89   *Badly damaged old St James' Church.*

authorities so much they would persuade the British gunners not to fire. If that was the idea, although disconcerting, it didn't work.

One of Dover's most ancient and historic churches, old St James' Church in Woolcomber Street, was wrecked by enemy action. On one occasion a missile in the churchyard threw up coffins and bodies of those buried years before. The church was badly damaged by a shell on 20 October 1940 which fell on the nearby St James' parish hall, killing Albert Ashbee, the landlord of the *Ancient Druid* public house, who was walking nearby. Even more damage was caused on 5 April 1943 when another shell fell in Woolcomber Street. There were hopes post-war that the church building would be repaired, but one night much of the damaged structure collapsed. It was feared there were people inside, but a search found this not to be so. Eventually Dover Borough Council decided to preserve the remains as a 'Tidy Ruin'.

Mrs Jean McBrien of Whitfield, then Jean King, remembers when she was about fourteen in 1943, cycling into Dover each day from her home at Lydden:

90   *Badly damaged old St James' Church from the churchyard.*

I was working at the time as a machinist at the Co-Operative Stores' tailoring department in the town centre in Biggin Street and when there was a raid, and there were plenty, we all had to troop down to the basement area for safety. On one occasion, I remember we were there all night. During that time the explosions were continuous and very loud. It was morning before we were able to emerge. I cycled down to my grandmother's house in Beach Street near the western docks for breakfast and recall that the roads, especially in Northampton Street and Snargate Street areas, were littered with broken glass and rubble following the raid. I couldn't ride my bike because of the rubble-strewn streets. The Market Square was a real mess. There was always a sentry, in his little box, on guard duty at The Viaduct checking if everyone had a good reason to go further towards the western docks. I was all right because I was visiting my grandmother and he just waved me through. I recall there was a garage on the right hand side of Snargate Street but that had been smashed.

The first night of May saw more shelling with nearly all the shells falling in the dock area, although one family in Union Road was saved by their Anderson shelter when a shell fell nearby. Early next morning a single shell landed in the Market Square, badly damaging Flashman's furniture store.

A week later, at Sunday teatime, two shells hit the town. One struck a house at the corner of Pencester Road and Maison Dieu Road, killing a man living in a ground-floor flat. His wife survived after being dug out of the debris. The other shell fell near the already badly damaged *Burlington Hotel*.

Ken Flint of Deal, a soldier tasked to work on communications under Dover Castle, recalls the brave spirit of Dovorians during the years of bombing and shelling:

> I was doing shift work under Dover Castle so that meant we were sometimes off duty during the daytime. It was wonderful to stroll along the streets of Dover and exchange smiles with passing civilians. They showed no signs at all of fear, despite 'Jerry' being only 21 miles away. The number of damaged properties in Dover demonstrated what the inhabitants were going through but nobody seemed to be frightened.

As the full moon approached in May the Germans stepped up their night raids on London, with bombers passing over Dover. The anti-aircraft guns were in action on several nights. One aircraft jettisoned its bombs with one landing at Temple Ewell.

The year's first bombs on the town came in the early hours of 22 May when one hit a row of houses in Mayfield Avenue at the top of Minerva Avenue. Six houses collapsed. Those killed were Charles Chapman, 52, his wife Louisa, 53, and their 17-year-old daughter, Doris. Another daughter was seriously injured. Further along the road Mrs Ivy Fussell, 49, also died. In all 13 people were taken to hospital and there was damage to property over a wide area. Eventually, 14 houses in Mayfield Avenue had to be demolished.

A whole month went by before there was further enemy action and for a complete week in early June there was not even an alert sounded. But early on 22 June a bomb was

91 *Dover Castle.*

92   *Corner of Cannon Street and Market Street was hit twice – in 1940 and 1943.*

dropped alongside the Prince of Wales' Pier, hitting a trawler which caught fire and injured six sailors.

On a sunny Sunday afternoon, on 27 June, only one of six shells hit Dover, but caused the highest casualty count for a single shell during the whole four years of bombardment. It fell in Cannon Street where a number of servicemen and women were strolling. Crashing down in the middle of the highway outside Burton's store, in seconds the street looked like a battlefield. Eleven servicemen, a member of the WRNS and a child were killed outright, while 21 service personnel and 10 civilians were taken to hospital. The little girl who lost her life was Rubina Streeter, 11, of Chapel Place.

Massive damage was caused to property in Cannon Street; signs of shrapnel damage can still be seen in the façades of some buildings. A huge hole in the road ruptured sewer pipes and underground services that took weeks to repair. The ruptured sewer gushed out water and other effluent that created a small pond in the centre of the highway that had to be cleared before repair work could get under way. To make matters worse, fire broke out in Burton's premises and the damage was so bad the property had to be demolished. It was reported at the time that a fragment of the shell was recovered from Balfour Road, more than a thousand yards away. Later in the week two salvage workers were nearly drowned when working in the flooded cellars of one of the nearby shops while trying to recover a valuable supply of sugar.

The Germans were evidently using heavier shells and this was proved the following night when one hit the General Post Office in Biggin Street. It landed on its roof and penetrated through into the telephone exchange, exploding with terrific force. Three telephone operators were killed. They were John Parfitt, George Kerry and Walter Garrett. Rescue operations were suspended when more shells began landing on the town, one causing further damage to the premises. Telephone equipment was wrecked and the town was without phone use for three weeks. Special arrangements were made for Civil Defence work and a temporary telephone exchange was set up in former tram sheds in Folkestone Road.

Another shell not far from the Post Office, in Priory Place, killed ambulance driver William Golding, 62, who was on duty with his ambulance trying to help those in the phone exchange. Five shells fired that June night killed four men and seriously injured another five.

In July only three shells from the German guns hit Dover. They caused no casualties and did very little damage. One of the shells again hit *Burlington Hotel*.

The Prime Minister was in Dover again on 17 July, this time with the United States Secretary for War, Edward Stimson, to visit the long-range guns near St Margaret's.

August opened with sultry weather and, in a thunderstorm, a German aircraft was seen to crash in flames into the sea off South Foreland. It was claimed as a 'kill' by the AA battery that had just arrived at Dover and officially confirmed. It brought the number of enemy aircraft destroyed by the Dover defences since the war started to nearly two hundred. No wonder German pilots called the Dover area Hellfire Corner.

93 *Post Office and Telephone Exchange shelled.*

Two Royal Navy officers were killed during an attack on 4 August when shells fell near the Crosswall at the western docks. Others fell in the Hillside Road area but caused only superficial damage. No civilians were injured.

The military and civilian authorities were concerned about the number of people ignoring the shelling warnings and continuing to walk the streets, resulting in a growing casualty list, so fresh instructions were issued that all military personnel and civilians must clear the streets when an alert was sounded.

Dover was shelled again on 24 August when six hit the town in daylight. Mrs Dorothy Gregory of East Street, Tower Hamlets, was killed by one shell that fell near her home. Three civilians were seriously injured. A woman serving in the Women's Auxiliary Air Force (WAAF) was badly wounded when one shell fell near the pavilion at Dover College sports ground where there was a barrage balloon site.

So ended the fourth year of war, during which 1,736 shells were recorded as falling on the town, nearly four times as many as high-explosive bombs. The number of alerts in four years was 2,707 in total.

At this time, as Allied troops invaded Italy, tougher restrictions were imposed on the freedom of residents and visitors to the area. This led to rumours that a Second Front (the invasion of the continent) was about to start. Actually it turned out to be a large-scale

94   *Priory Gate Road hit.*

95 *The National Fire Service in action.*

amphibious exercise in the English Channel, in preparation for D-Day. Large numbers of troops were drafted into the Dover area and a number of roads were closed to traffic except army lorries and tanks. In the Channel a fleet of naval vessels took part in the exercise in daylight on 9 September and were completely unmolested by German guns.

Later in September there was regular shelling of Dover with sporadic firing, and on 15 September there was heavy anti-aircraft gunfire when German planes crossed the coast. One was seen to go down in flames into the sea and the Air Ministry claimed this was attacked by an RAF night fighter. Bombs were dropped over a wide area of East Kent, including some in Thanet.

German guns were in action again on 25 September and shells landed near Fremlins' brewery (off the Market Square), and in Pencester Road on a derelict site where a bomb had wrecked the property in 1942.

October brought more shells and resulted in more deaths in Dover. Often the shelling attacks were in retaliation for British long-range guns firing at German shipping creeping along the French coast.

There was heavy shelling on 3 October when the tobacconist's shop at the corner of Queen Street and Bench Street, owned by Jack Williams, later a Conservative mayor of the town, was badly damaged and later demolished. Fire broke out because the shell fractured a gas main in the highway. Members of the National Fire Service (NFS) were soon fighting the blaze and their efforts continued while more shells were falling on the town. The English traitor, Lord Haw Haw, speaking on German radio, claimed their gunners on the French coast could see the blaze, which he claimed was among dock installations.

There were eight shells that night causing considerable damage, including the public toilets in Gaol Lane (off the Market Square), the previously blitzed Dover museum and the town's covered market underneath. Howard Andrews, a director of Chitty's Mill and the town's Fire Guard Officer, was knocked down by the blast of the shell that fell in Gaol Lane.

96   Guildhall Vaults *hit.*

Destroyed in this attack was the *Guildhall Vaults*, one of the oldest public houses in Dover, being founded in 1690. This stood roughly on the site of the old town gaol and court and it was believed at one time a secret tunnel ran from the Vaults to the Western Heights for the removal of prisoners. The crater caused by the explosion, however, produced no sign of this reputed tunnel.

The corporation's public baths near the Town Hall were wrecked when the shell narrowly missed the council's debating chamber. Flashman's furniture depository in Dieu Stone Lane (next to St Mary's Church), already damaged by splinters, was wrecked.

97   *Flashman's furniture depository destroyed.*

98   *St Barnabas Church was damaged and never repaired.*

Around this time the Germans began dropping 'butterfly bombs' over East Kent. They were interesting objects to be found, especially for children who were intrigued by the wings to the missiles that made them look like big butterflies.

Walter Bates, receiving lessons at St Bartholomew's School after his own St Martin's School had been damaged, remembers sadly what happened to one group of lads:

> My close mates had discovered this brightly coloured object on the hills. They shut themselves in the school toilets to examine it. The object exploded in their faces. It was a booby trap bomb. One lad lost a hand and his eyesight for ever, another lost an eye, others were badly scarred. I would have been with them except my father had sent me on an errand. After that explosion the police toured schools warning of the danger of picking up these deadly bombs. We did not need telling twice.

99   *Coombe Valley Road during the war.*

On 17 October there was more shelling as the enemy fired at Allied minesweepers in the Channel. There was plenty of air activity over Dover on 19 and 23 October with anti-aircraft guns in action on both nights.

In the four months since the GPO was hit only three people had lost their lives through enemy action, but on 25 October nine shells on Dover killed six and seriously injured another nine. Most of the shells on this occasion fell in the Buckland area and military sources suggested that this was because the Germans had fitted new barrels to their guns, overshooting as a result.

One shell crashed down on a house in Glenfield Road, killing four members of one family. They were: Mrs Alice Shearne, 38, Alice Shearne, 15, Joan Shearne, 13, and Brenda Shearne, three. Another woman, Mrs Phoebe Payne, 59, was also killed.

Other shells landed in Cherry Tree Avenue, where a vehicle was set on fire, and on a large house in London Road being used by Customs and Excise who had moved there when Barton Road Infants' School was required for teaching purposes. They had to move once again, this time to Folkestone Road. This shell killed George Hill of Wimbledon, who, was returning to his lodging when the missile landed, damaging the Regent Picture Palace opposite (the site is now the army recruiting centre).

October ended with three nights of air activity but no bombs were dropped. Dover anti-aircraft guns were in action on all three nights.

The worst incident in the last two months of the year was on 2 November when 10 shells landed on Dover. Two people were killed and seven taken to hospital. Houses in Glenfield Road again suffered where Alfred Jenkins, 67, was killed. One shell landed close to damaged St Barnabas Church (now the site of Barton Road School's playing field) near where one of the war's first shells had landed. Another fell in Northampton Street where Mrs Margaret Licence, 72, was killed.

During the morning of 2 December a German aircraft flew over the town, under the cover of low cloud, but passing over St Margaret's Bay was shot down in to the sea by an alert gun crew.

Two days later British gunners opened up on enemy shipping, firing about fifty rounds, and the Germans retaliated for about twenty minutes but no shells landed in the town.

Two days before Christmas there was heavy shelling from the guns at Cap Gris Nez and Calais, with hits on Folkestone and Deal and only two on Dover. One of those shells hit the former Congregational Church and Sunday School in Russell Street causing so much damage the building had to be demolished.

The *Dover Express* reported that by the end of 1943 there had been 151 civilians killed in the town as a result of enemy action, of which 48 were as the result of enemy shelling. The number of civilians seriously injured was just over 300 with another 200 slightly injured.

1944

The Tide of War Turning

THE TIDE OF war in 1944 was turning in the Allies' favour and a few people in Dover were thinking their ordeal of bombing and shelling would soon be over. They were in for a shock.

On 2 January 1944, a single enemy aircraft flying over the town met with heavy anti-aircraft gunfire and crashed in flames at Oxney near the Dover-Deal road. During the next fortnight the sirens sounded only four times but there were no incidents.

Over the next few weeks the procedure was often the same. British guns would fire at enemy shipping creeping along the French coast and a few minutes later the German gunners would retaliate. It was officially announced that the gunners at St Margaret's had hit and sunk a large enemy ship off the French coast.

In one of the January attacks a shell fell on a shelter at Deal where 14 people were killed. One of the shells that hit Dover landed in the grammar school's playing field at Astor Avenue.

Bombed out of their home in Percival Terrace, the Bates family moved to Church Road, where young Walter had another narrow escape. He recalls:

> Early in the year a shell landed at the back of our home in Church Road. Mum and I were on our way out of the front door to a shelter in the crypt of St Martin's Church nearby, when the shell blew every window out of the house. If we had remained in the house we would have been cut to shreds by flying glass. Our luck was with us yet again.

The enemy launched a heavy air attack on London and other cities in January, in retaliation for a bombing raid by the RAF on Berlin. A fleet of 90 Luftwaffe planes headed for London, some passing over Dover, and a third of them never made it back to their bases. One of the aircraft was brought down by Dover guns and crashed on the Western Heights where it burned brightly for half an hour with ammunition exploding. By the time the fire was out there was virtually nothing left of the aircraft.

This was almost the last throw of the Luftwaffe as a long-range bombing force over the United Kingdom. It was a landmark day for Dover on 22 January when it received the last bombs dropped by an enemy piloted aircraft. (Dover was hit by four bombs on 3 June, but these were found to have been dropped by the RAF. They landed harmlessly on the foreshore.)

These last German bombs, a stick of 11, killed two and injured seven. Stanhope Road, which received considerable damage throughout the war, was hit by one of the bombs, which brought down two houses. Families in their Morrison shelters at home had lucky escapes, but Thomas Godsmark, 64, a shelter marshal, was dead when dug out of the debris. Baby Valerie Hemming died from injuries a few days later.

This last air raid was followed by a week without incident, but on 22 January our guns started firing across the Channel and the enemy returned fire. None of the enemy shells fell on the town but one fell in the rural area where a number of WAAF personnel were sleeping, causing 26 casualties. Two of the women died.

February proved to be a relatively quiet month in the south east, but in one raid a shell fell on the RAF camp at Swingate where a number of WAAF women were injured.

Throughout March there were a series of sea battles in the Channel off Dover, with Dover-based MTBs attacking enemy shipping off the French coast. On occasions these battles were backed up by shelling by both sides.

Roy Eddy of Ontario, Canada, remembers those sea battles:

> I was 20 at the time serving as a radar officer on a frigate of the Royal Canadian Navy. We were operating with the Royal Navy, out of Portsmouth where we replenished our supplies. We sailed for the French coast where we joined in the bombardment of Boulogne where our mission was to destroy installations in the harbour. All the time we were being shelled by the enemy guns on the coast. It was quite a noisy mission.

Allied air superiority was very evident by this time with large numbers of British and American aircraft flying over Dover towards France and Germany and only the occasional flight over the Kent coast by a German aircraft.

The first shelling casualties in Dover for four months came on 20 March during yet another duel between the British and German long-range guns. Scores of shells were exchanged and one hit two homes in Prioress Walk where two children, Donald and Maureen Smillie, aged seven and five, were killed.

At the Grand Shaft Barracks on the Western Heights one shell killed an army captain and a quartermaster sergeant, both serving in the South Staffordshire Regiment. On this day one shell wrecked the *Wheelwright Arms* in Bridge Street and another demolished old buildings in Chapel Lane, off Snargate Street, next door to the *Dover Express* offices where the printing presses had a narrow escape.

Many shells fell around St Margaret's, where the British guns had been located, and one shell cut the town's electricity supply, leaving Dover without power for several hours.

100   *Grand Shaft Barracks.*

Norman Sutton, in his war diary, noted that it was pretty obvious in Dover that the Second Front (the invasion of France) was approaching:

> Dover became a Regulated Area within which certain restrictions were imposed. The use of telescopes and binoculars was banned and the seafront area was closed to the public, except for those with special passes. The ban was announced on 8 April and by the 20th large tall barriers had been erected at New Bridge, Woolcomber Street, St James' Street and anywhere that had access to the seafront. What went on behind the barriers was not apparent but rumours were rife.

While this was going on Dover was experiencing a relatively quiet time – the calm before the storm.

There was air activity over south-east England on several nights in early April, and on 20 April there was another exchange of fire by the long-range guns with four shells landing on the town. One landed on Thomas's ironmonger's shop in King Street and another in Pencester Gardens on the banks of the river.

May opened with increasing air activity by Allied aircraft and in the first weeks of the month there were tremendous explosions heard in Dover from across the water in Nord-Pas de Calais. Later, Dover people discovered this was an all-out attempt to destroy the German flying bomb sites before the Germans had a chance to fire them.

One of the heaviest raids was on 9 May when on three occasions there were such heavy explosions from the French coast that houses in Dover shook.

More huge explosions from Northern France were heard in Dover when, on 19 June the RAF's 19 Lancaster bombers of 617 Squadron dropped 12,000lb Tallboy bombs on the V2 rocket storage and experimental site at Watten near St Omer. The Lancasters flew in at 500 feet to ensure they wrecked the area surrounding the dome-like concrete structure built into the hillside.

These were especially dangerous times in Dover. Mrs Jean McBrien remembers:

> If you were in Dover when the siren went you had to go to the nearest shelter. I was cycling home to Lydden one afternoon and had got as far as Buckland School in London Road when the siren began to wail. I put my foot down on the pedals a bit smartish in order to get out of Dover before I was stopped. I just made it to the boundary which was Buckland Mill.
>   At home on one occasion we heard a noise like a motor bike in the sky. We rushed outside and saw an odd looking plane flying over our heads. My dad said: 'Look the plane has its tail on fire.' It was one of the first doodle bugs.

There was shelling on only two days in May. On 19 May German shells fell in the sea off Dover and on 23 May the British guns at St Margaret's opened fire on enemy shipping. They fired 30 shells and the enemy replied very swiftly but none of their 10 shells fell on Dover. For nearly a month the guns were not heard again.

By the end of May it was evident that the Second Front was only weeks or days away. In the country around Dover there were signs of a massive build up of war materiel.

For those who had passes and could get on to the seafront they could see landing barges tied up to the buoys in the harbour, but few realised they were dummy craft, made from painted cloth stretched over a framework and floated on barrels, to fool the Germans into

101   *Dummy craft.*

102 *Montgomery in 1946 when granted the Freedom of Dover.*

believing the landings would be in the Calais area with Dover as an invasion base.

These dummy tank landing craft were mostly constructed in Dover Harbour Board workshops, now the premises of the Cullen's Yard bistro, and then silently wheeled at night to the harbour and launched from a concrete apron opposite the Granville Gardens.

Dover and East Kent played a major role in this deception of the enemy, code-named Operation Fortitude. One of the main tricks was the use of 'turned' captured Nazi spies which MI5 had persuaded to work for the Allies. One radioed disinformation to his German contact that he had been informed by a friend in Dover of a big build up of troops around the town. This, of course, was not true but it helped to create a picture that encouraged Hitler to believe the Allied invasion would be from Dover and Folkestone on Pas de Calais.

Troops around Dover sent out bogus messages on their units' radios, picked up by German listening posts on the French coast that gave the impression of a massive military build up.

Field Marshal Montgomery added to the hoax by visiting Dover where he even held a meeting in the Town Hall to discuss how the local authorities would be able to cope with the many bodies expected to be washed ashore as a result of the landing near Calais.

Joe Harman, by now in the Home Guard, was instructed to learn to ride a motorbike and told to take a trip into the country:

> I rode out to Lydden and turned along the quiet Swanton Lane where I knew there was an emergency airfield. When I approached the airfield, planes suddenly swooped down as though attacking it. I nearly fell off my motor bike and quickly turned round and made off back to Dover. It was only later I discovered this air activity involved only a few planes, taking off and landing to create a blip on the enemy radar to give the impression of a build up of forces ready to invade the French coast around Calais.

More aprons and small piers were constructed at East Cliff to add to the deception of the enemy. It was feared the Germans, thinking these were for loading troops onto the landing craft, might smother the area in mustard gas. Just in case, members of the Home Guard were trained, on top of their other duties, how to decontaminate the area.

On the first days of June huge strange-looking objects were seen being towed past Dover. They were parts of the Mulberry harbours sunk off the Normandy coast after the D-Day invasion took place on 6 June. Amazingly, although visibility was good, the German gunners never fired at these strange objects. They were reserving their ammunition for the expected invasion on the coast near Calais, across the narrowest point of the English Channel. The deception in which Dover played its part succeeded.

One action in which Dover seafarers took part was when the cruiser HMS *Albatross* went aground on the Goodwin Sands and was attacked by the Luftwaffe, but strangely the German guns took no part. The Dover tug, *Lady Brassey*, sailed to the scene escorted by HMS *Lois*, while six enemy aircraft appeared out of the clouds and tried to drop bombs on what must have been a sitting target. The bombs fell on either side of the helpless cruiser but failed to damage the ship. After six hours, with the help of *Lady Brassey* and the other Dover tug *Lady Duncannon*, the cruiser was hauled off the Sands on the rising tide after 40 tons of ballast were removed. The cruiser was then able to continue its voyage down the Channel under its own power.

On 6 June came the news that the Allies had landed on the coast of Normandy. It was D-Day. The long-awaited Second Front had begun. In the next few weeks large convoys were seen passing Dover on their way to the invasion beaches. Some days the German

103   Lady Brassey *tug.*

104 Maid of Orleans.

gunners shelled them, but on other days the convoys were just ignored. It is estimated that from D-Day to the capture of the long-range guns near Calais, a period of about four months, 1,000 ships, some of 10,000 tons, passed through the Strait just off the harbour. Losses were practically negligible. If there was shelling, smoke screens were created by their escorting destroyers and by fast motor boats which dashed to mid-Channel and put down smoke floats.

One of the rare successes by the German gunners was on D-Day when a large convoy was passing Dover. A large ship, the SS *Sambut*, was hit and caught fire. Despite efforts by fire-fighters the ship was finally abandoned. Eighteen soldiers on board were killed as well as one member of the ship's crew. Many more were injured and the survivors were landed at Dover.

Among the 4,000 ships taking part in the D-Day landings were Dover cross-Channel ferries, including the *Maid of Orleans* with its master, Captain Len Payne. The vessel carried thousands of troops to the Normandy bridgehead. A few weeks later the *Maid of Orleans*, this time under Captain Masters, was sunk while on the way to the bridgehead.

Convoys continued to pass through the Strait and by mid-June were regularly shelled. In one shelling, on 7 June, a dozen shells fell on Dover when Stephen Jenkins, 72, of Clarendon Place was killed and more than twenty civilians injured as well as a number of soldiers.

Later the same day there was more shelling when John Mullane, 64, was killed when one fell at Albany Place. Another shell crashed down in front of St Martin's House at the corner of Effingham Street and Folkestone Road, a centre used by the YMCA. Several voluntary workers were injured and taken to hospital.

For the next five days convoys sailed up and down the Channel with no shells being fired and this silence, although not realised in Dover at the time, might have been caused by preparations to launch a new secret weapon, the V1 Flying Bomb.

The first of these flying bombs, or buzz bombs or doodlebugs as they became known, crossed the Kent coast in the Romney Marsh district about 4 a.m. on Tuesday 13 June. This 'secret weapon' might have been a surprise to many in Dover, but not to the Allies' military authorities who had ordered bombing raids on the launching sites for several weeks.

As a result of the arrival of these terror weapons there was a massive redeployment of anti-aircraft defences along the coast, with more guns and crews switched to the Dover area. American gun crews were among those who arrived.

American anti-aircraft gunners, high on the cliffs overlooking Dover, played a major role in the defence of the town against enemy flying bombs in 1944. During their time near Dover, four members of their battalion were killed and seven wounded by enemy shelling.

It was on the night of 29 July that the US 127 AAA Gun Battalion moved in to their new camp on the cliffs of Dover and within four days its members were in firing positions at what they called Camp Swingate. During their six weeks on Dover cliffs the Americans shared slit trenches, foxholes and firing missions with the British gunners, all determined to shoot down buzz bombs before they crossed the coast.

105   V1 (Doodlebug).

During that short time the battalion, known as the Screaming Eagles, engaged 188 flying bombs (V1s), firing more than 6,000 rounds of 90mm shells, claiming 89 shot down and were allowed 56 of them. Part of their success was that the battalion was using the latest proximity fuse, known to the troops as Bonzos.

Their guns were situated close to the Swingate masts and not far from the British-manned 15-inch guns, and so were in the target zone for the German gunners. As a result the battalion was hit by German shells on a number of occasions. Charles Vulyak, son of a member of the battalion based at Dover, wrote in The Dover Society's newsletter:

> The battalion had more casualties while defending the south east of England and London from the V1s than during any battle campaign on the Continent of Europe.

On 27 September the battalion crossed the Channel from Southampton to Omaha Beach to begin their next big assignment of helping to free Europe of tyranny.

The bravery of the American gunners, some of whom died defending Dover, is recognised in a memorial that stands just off the Dover to St Margaret's road not far from where their guns once fired. American visitors regularly visit the spot to pay homage to their countrymen who died in a foreign field.

As Dover was not in the direct flight line of many of these erratic flying bombs, the town escaped lightly compared with many areas of Kent and London. Walter Bates remembers their arrival:

> My dad and I watched the first of these weapons on a bright moonlit night while we stood outside the crypt of St Martin's Church where we sheltered from bombing and shelling. We could not believe our eyes when this plane came through, very low, illuminated by searchlights and with ack-ack fire bursting all around. Later we discovered it had no pilot. In a few days the Germans were sending over hundreds of these doodlebugs.

Only three of these terror weapons crashed down within Dover's boundary throughout the war, one of which flew so low it crashed into Shakespeare Cliff. The other two came down near gun sites at Lydden Spout.

To add to the terror the enemy brought into use a more high-powered gun, sending shells into Folkestone and even as far away as Maidstone, some sixty miles from the French coast. It was the only time this new type of gun was used. Barry Fincham remembers well those terrible days:

> Shelling of the town during late August and September was intense. In one day in September more than 50 shells fell in the town. We stayed and slept in the deep air-raid shelters in Buckland Mill grounds. But the Canadians finally captured the German long-range guns and for all of us it felt like peace at last.

Day and night the throb of the flying bombs could be heard crossing the Channel. At night flames from the back of the buzz bombs could be clearly seen.

The newly sited AA guns and the RAF working together brought down scores of the bombs as they approached the coast to the west of Dover, but some got through and caused thousands of deaths in London and its environs.

Meanwhile the steady stream of Allied convoys continued through the Strait with the ships on the way to the Normandy beachhead where there was desperate fighting. Enemy shelling of the convoys continued and on 20 June one ship was hit and set on fire. A more determined shelling attack followed on 24 June when the *Empire Lough* was hit and so badly damaged the ship was beached off Abbots Cliff where it burned for several days. The vessel was loaded with cans of petrol for the troops in Normandy and as the ship burned the cans burst and were flung far and wide.

More shelling at a convoy followed the next day, and on 26 June one of the shells overshot and landed on Dover seafront near the damaged sea baths. A contingent of the Royal Army Medical Corps, sent to Dover to deal with the expected number of wounded troops, was watching the attack on the passing convoy. Three of the medics were killed and 13 seriously injured.

One of the other shells hit the collier *Dalegarth Force*, killing three of the crew. The convoy's escort put down a smoke screen and under cover of this the ship was towed into Dover harbour. Later the same day, two more shells were fired at Dover, one of which fell at the back of the already-wrecked Salvation Army headquarters while the other crashed down on London Road causing considerable damage, but there were no casualties. This time is remembered by Barry Fincham:

> Frequent shelling from the German guns in Pas de Calais was by now a regular occurrence with most nights disturbed and spent in the shelters. One frightful aspect of shelling was that a shell had to fall before the sirens were sounded and people could take shelter. In Buckland a fore warning of shelling was to hear the hooters of the army diesel trains that were used to haul the shells for our long-range guns hidden in the Guston railway tunnel. We knew that when our guns fired the Germans would retaliate. About this time a shell fell at the back of our house and badly damaged the rear half. Our family had taken refuge under the stairs. We had been too frightened to run to the shelter at Buckland School.

Sixty shells were fired at a convoy on 29 June, without causing any damage, and four shells fell on Dover and in the rural area near the town.

Throughout July enemy shelling was not so frequent despite convoys continuing to pass through the Strait on the way to Normandy. This was partly due to a ruse thought up by the Royal Navy which put down smoke screens off Dover when there was no convoy due. At first the German gunners assumed there was a convoy and began shelling, but their guns were not ready when the ships actually began to sail through the Strait. Eventually the German gunners realised what was going on and slowed down the rate of fire.

Although flying bombs continued to cross the Channel in growing numbers with more and more being shot down, the German guns remained silent until 23 July when they aimed at a convoy but were too late. The ships had already passed through the dangerous

106   *A captured German U-boat U776 in Dover Harbour.*

stretch of water. Shells fell at St Margaret's and shops at the top of Bay Hill were wrecked. The only other shelling was on 26 July, but once again the convoys were clear of the Strait by nearly an hour.

Shells were not the only danger to ships in the English Channel. German E-boats were in action on 27 July when torpedoes were fired and two ships were hit. In the darkness the Dover pilot cutter *Pioneer* picked up 35 survivors off Dungeness.

August proved another quiet month from shelling for Dover and it was not until 29 August that the town was hit, although five shells fell outside the harbour earlier in the month.

By mid-August the Germans were in full retreat in France as the Allies broke out of the Normandy bridgehead, and there were those in Dover who thought their ordeal would soon be over. Canadian and British troops were fighting their way more slowly along the coast towards the German long-range guns near Boulogne and Calais, but while the enemy retreated through France there was no sign they were prepared to abandon these guns.

To prove the point, on 29 August the German guns began their final bombardment of Dover that was to prove the worst ordeal the town suffered throughout the war. Barry Fincham again:

> Shelling in 1944 was becoming more intense. I remember Old Park Barracks about this time was full of American GIs and French Canadians as well as members of British regiments. The GIs were extremely generous and a great favourite with the children. They were always willing to give us gum and other sweets. The black American troops were especially nice and would always be interesting to talk to and listen to our news.

The German gunners, who must have known their days were numbered, decided to cause as much damage as they could in Dover and other towns before they were forced to surrender. They seemed determined to use as much ammunition as they could before the capture of their guns.

Peter Bean of Whitfield, who had left Dover County School in evacuation, was working as a junior clerk in Barclays Bank in Dover's Cannon Street. He remembers many scary incidents:

107   *Corner of Cannon Street and Market Square ruined.*

> The most terrifying came in August 1944, after D-Day, when the Allied forces were approaching the guns on the French coast. For several weeks Dover was subjected to the worst period of constant shelling, day and night. On many occasions it was necessary for those working in the bank to spend much of the day, and the night, in the bank's basement strong room.
>
> When the shelling warning was in operation we were not allowed to leave the building. Sometimes we could not leave to go home until 4.30 in the morning when I would cycle home to Whitfield, have a quick wash and breakfast and return to the bank to start work again on the same day at 9am.
>
> In late August 1944 we were sheltering in the bank's strong room at about 2.30 p.m., having just enjoyed a meal of a tin of hot soup, when the whole building was shaken by a huge explosion and we were left in complete darkness. A shell had landed in Cannon Street, just outside the bank premises. The empty rooms over the bank were brought down and the bank itself was in ruins. It was just possible to get out of the building through an emergency exit at the back of the property. Fortunately none of the bank staff of four was injured. But that was not the case in the street outside. Several servicemen were killed, having just left the Plaza cinema which had to be evacuated when the shell warning was given. We were unable to continue trading from the bank premises so we moved all the cash and the ledgers to the Midland Bank further up the town where we stayed until October 1944 while our bank was temporarily repaired.
>
> It must be unique to have rival banks trading at either end of the same counter, but such was the spirit and cooperation in friendly Dover at that time of the war.

The next month there followed 'a whirlwind, sadistic orgy of destruction', as described by Norman Sutton. Enormous damage was caused to the already stricken town. During the greatest intensity of shelling, in the second and third weeks of September, Dover became a town under siege with business life forced to a virtual standstill. Shops closed, schools failed to re-open after the summer holidays and hundreds of people remained

108   *Chittenden's basement
bread shop.*

109   *Business as usual on
the whelk stall.*

FRONT-LINE TOWN: And Then A Warning On

in shelters for days on end. In large sectors of the town there were no deliveries of bread and milk for two or three days. One of the larger bakeries in the town was put out of action for several days. Life got so bad that the Ministry of Food sent food into the town. Hot soup and other meals were prepared on mobile kitchen vehicles and passed down to the hungry people in shelters. Reviewing the situation, Norman Sutton, commented:

> The very intensity of the brutal attacks probably helped to reduce the number of casualties. Dover people realised the German gunners were determined to vent spite to their frustration and cause as much damage as they could before they fell before the inexorable advance of the Allied armies. That being so, Dovorians did the sensible thing and took cover until the guns were finally silenced. Casualties were by no means light, but in view of the enormous damage caused the deaths might have been many more.

Not all could take cover and remain under cover. The men and women of the Civil Defence were kept busy while the shells rained down. This force included air-raid wardens, rescue personnel, repair squads, drivers, police and ambulance staff.

The bombardment of 29 August sent about thirty shells, of which nine fell in the town, causing the death of Alice Marjoram, 61, at St Andrew's Terrace. Six people were wounded and taken to hospital.

In the previous eight months only six civilians had been killed by shelling, which made some people think that the worst was over. They were soon to be disillusioned. After two days' rest the German guns opened up again and began heavy shelling in bright moonlight early on 1 September. Three or four guns opened up at about the same time and for four hours the firing continued without interruption. More than 100 shells screamed across the Channel. Of these nearly 40 fell on Dover or the harbour, more in the rural area, 22 on Ramsgate and five at Folkestone.

110 *Hard-pressed Civil Defence workers.*

One of the first shells fired that September morning struck the entrance to the Lagoon Cave in Dover's High Street where four people were killed. They were caught hurrying to the shelter. Altogether eight civilians died in the town during this heavy spell of shelling. Those killed at the shelter were: Mabel Hubbard, 54, of *The Globe Inn* on Peter Street, Ellen Mills, 39, of Peter Street and her daughter, Yvonne, four, and Charles Benbow, 52, of the Metropole Flats. In the Tower Hamlets area Lydia Ricketts, 43, died from her injuries while Sheila Hare, six, was killed. At Kearsney, in Pavilion Meadow, Robert Wheeler, 54, was fatally injured and another to die was William Cook, 67, of Military Road.

On 2 September Dover experienced one of the most bitter cross-Channel gun duels of the war. The action began just before midnight when the British guns near St Margaret's opened fire on enemy shipping trying to evacuate Calais and Boulogne before the

111   *Another rescue by Civil Defence workers.*

advancing Canadian troops arrived. Several enemy craft trying to escape the French ports were intercepted by Allied light craft of the Royal Navy, the Royal Canadian Navy and the Dutch navy. Then the British guns and the RAF joined in the attack. The British gunners

112   *Civil Defence feeding centre.*

113   *Clarence Place, Pier District.*

114   *Chitty's Mill pre-war.*

fired 220 rounds and, reported the War Department, sank five craft trying to get away from Boulogne and six ships in other German convoys. When one trawler went to the aid of a sinking vessel the British gunners sank them both.

The German gunners took up the challenge and soon shells were falling around St Margaret's. Only four of the 150 German shells crashed down on Dover, but one led to the destruction through fire of Chitty's flour mill at Charlton. The missile set fire to a lorry that started the blaze, resulting in the destruction of a large amount of machinery and grain. Damage was estimated at half a million pounds and the mill, for many years a good employer, never re-opened.

The *Dover Express* reported that 1 September was the last day of buzz bomb attacks from the Calais area, but one was brought down at Alkham causing damage to power lines, resulting in Dover being without electricity for several hours.

The anniversary of the outbreak of the war, on 3 September, saw the German guns fire around a hundred shells. One fell on the ferry dock at the western docks, killing a naval officer and injuring four ratings. There were at least 10 airbursts over the town, showering down shrapnel.

Each day there were duels between the guns on the coasts 21 miles apart. On 11 September one shell fell on Dodds Place where Agnes Hart, a 73-year-old widow, was trapped and later found dead.

More shells hit Dover the following day and people on their way home were caught in the streets. Killed outside Christ Church (now the site of a block of flats) in Folkestone Road were Christopher Wade, 78, Ernest McGuire, 15, and NFS officer Herbert Dowell

115   *Chitty's Mill destroyed.*

of Barry who had been sent to help out Dover firemen. Church verger Albert Bussey, 68, died in hospital from his injuries.

Another shell fell in Dickson Road among a group of six Anderson shelters, two of which were within two feet of the crater. Three more people were killed in this explosion: Kathleen Hogben, 36, and her son Harold, 16, and Mrs Rose Staveley, 60, all from Dickson Road.

A soldier and an RAF man lost their lives that night making a total death toll of seven. In addition 25 people were seriously injured.

There was a very vicious bombardment on 13 September which lasted five hours, with six guns employed. One of the first shells of this attack fell just outside the Priory Station, turning the scene into something like a battlefield. A train had just arrived and the passengers were streaming out of the station. Many were seriously injured and five were killed. Among those who lost their lives at the station were: Julia Green, 61, nine-year-old Fred Spinner, two servicemen and an Auxiliary Territorial Service (ATS) girl.

More shells began falling on the town and for many hours the majority of the townsfolk who were not on duty remained under cover, saving many lives. Twenty-three shells fell on the borough at varying intervals, one killing William Champion, 55, and another killing Thomas Doherty who lived in Gravesend. One shell, probably of the armour-piercing type, wrecked Boots at the corner of Worthington Street, going through the roof of the next but one property and then passing through the adjoining shop before exploding in the basement of Boots. No-one was in the building. Another shell fell at Kearsney where John Price of Margate was killed. By the time the 'All Clear' was sounded the shelling had been in progress for nearly eleven hours and nine people had lost their lives.

The next day, 14 September, the warnings were in operation for 17 hours and Dover was reaching the stage where normal life was becoming impossible. Yet the postmen were able to make at least one delivery of letters each day while telegrams were delivered when the opportunity occurred. Telephone operators at the GPO reported many subscribers were ringing up to find which day of the week it was. The incessant attacks had caused them to lose count of time.

Shelling continued all day, bringing businesses to a standstill, and emergency food arrangements were made to feed people sheltering in the caves. For the only occasion throughout the war, the *Dover Express* missed its Friday publication and was forced to come out a day late.

On Friday 15 September, more shelling warnings sent people to their shelters, this time for 14 hours. Norman Sutton noted:

> The discipline of Dover people seeking shelter and remaining there greatly reduced the casualties. Only four people were slightly injured during the long bombardment that day. But the continued bombardment was beginning to have an effect on those townspeople who, deluded by stories of the cessation of shelling, had returned to Dover.

Shells falling that day were strewn over a wide area with many of them falling between Dover and Folkestone during the day but, when darkness came, the German gunners concentrated on Dover. The area around Beaconsfield Road with its junction with London Road received half a dozen shells. One wrecked the Methodist Chapel schoolroom which had been used as a rest centre for those made homeless due to enemy action.

By the second week of September the shelling had become intense and so prolonged that it became impossible for milk and bread roundsmen to make their deliveries. Sheltering Dovorians began to go without their normal food. Norman Sutton again:

> In his final desperate efforts, the enemy was at last achieving a noticeable effect upon the town's civilian population that he had failed to do during four long years of shelling.

The swift advance of the Allied armies across France had, by 18 September, allowed the British authorities to lift the complete black-out in parts of Great Britain where street lights were switched on for the first time in five years. But, of course, this did not apply to the Dover area where lights could be seen from the German-occupied French coast.

In Dover there was no let up in the shelling and many Dover people, still in their shelters, went without milk for the fourth day.

During that black month of September BBC broadcaster Audrey Russell toured Dover and told of the fortitude of the town's people:

> We drove round the town and looked at the damage. Indeed Dover is a sorry sight. Nearly every house has windows boarded up, most of them have no glass at all. Nearly every wall bears the marks of shell splinters and there's much devastation and complete ruin. Two more shells have just crashed into Dover's streets. The Civil Defence workers are shovelling up the bricks and mortar and glass. People have come from all over town to try to find out if their friends have been injured. Already there's a mobile kitchen, operated by the WVS who are giving out tea to the people suffering from shock. But everything is under control and it's quite incredible how light the people make of their troubles. Someone said to me just now 'Well, they're used to it.' Luckily there are no fatal casualties this time. People are going around saying 'Well, it might have been worse.' I am afraid that incidents like this are daily occurrences in life just now in Dover.

As the Canadians and British advanced along the French coast, the long-range guns around Dover fired many rounds in support with their shells falling around the German coastal batteries. In Dover on Saturday 16 September, expecting further retaliation, the population kept under cover for a total of more than seventeen hours.

There were shorter periods of shelling on the following Sunday, Monday and Tuesday. On that day the Allies captured Boulogne and advanced along the coast to Cap Gris Nez and Calais where several of the long-range guns were in fortified positions.

It was then that the Germans decided to make their final fling with their big guns. The enemy gunners, hemmed in on all sides, increased the fury of the attacks, creating for Dover one of the most savage episodes of the war.

116   *Women's
Voluntary Service
loading up.*

The first shell in this final assault fell on Saturday 23 September, crashing into the Salvation
Army Red Shield canteen in Snargate Street, exploding low down and bringing the whole
building crashing down on those inside. Five civilians, all helpers, were killed. They were
45-year-old Salvation Army captain Bill Aspinall, who had helped scores of townsfolk and
military in Dover during the previous few months, supervisor Muriel Goldup, 44, Betty
Bushell, 20, Isabella Simpson, 47, all of Dover, and Ruth Berry, 23, of Torquay, a mobile

117   *WVS mobile kitchen.*

118   *Red Star Club, Snargate Street, destroyed.*

canteen driver. The bodies of two service people were also recovered from the debris. Nine civilians who lived nearby and a soldier were seriously injured and 10 more slightly hurt.

Civil Defence, military and naval working parties carried on digging into the debris for 19 hours seeking survivors. A small fire broke out in the ruins and was dealt with by the NFS While this rescue work was in progress more shells fell on Dover; one just missed Constable's Tower in Dover Castle.

The next day, 24 September, proved to be a relatively quiet day, but it preceded 48 hours of the most destructive time that Dover endured during the war. Many businesses closed; there was a problem supplying food and, for the first time, morale collapsed for several days.

There were two bouts of shelling on 25 September and in each case, as usual, the first shell arrived before the siren warnings could be given. The first shell of the second bombardment caused a terrible tragedy. Women, out for a few hours attempting to do their shopping, were caught without warning in London Road near Cherry Tree Avenue. Three of them and a child were killed and six others injured. Those who lost their lives through this shell were: Doris Buddle, 26, Mabel Wakefield, 59, Ellen Sydenham, 30, and seven-year-old Patricia Perkins. Ronald Chapman, 17, died later in hospital from his injuries. The main road was closed for several days because of the damage.

Another shell fell near the *Red Cow* in Folkestone Road (roughly where the York Street roundabout is now) making a huge crater in the highway and causing so much damage to underground services that they were not fully repaired until December. This shell killed Adeline Busswell, 64, whose body was not found for 48 hours. She is believed to have dived into a doorway for shelter on her way home to Eaton Road.

On the same day another shell fell right in the middle of the bowling green in Maison Dieu Gardens, near the Town Hall, causing a crater 40 feet across. The next shell crashed down on Edred Road, killing Elizabeth Wilson, 50, who lived there.

The death toll that day was seven, while 11 others in Dover were seriously injured.

The Royal Hippodrome announced that it would close for the following week, but a 16-inch German shell on Monday 25 September 1944 wrote the final chapter in the life of Dover's popular theatre in Snargate Street that had provided so much entertainment for soldiers, sailors and civilians throughout the war.

119   *Marine Station was hit several times on 25 September 1944.*

The theatre, built from public subscriptions by a group of wealthy Dovorians in 1790, opened as the Clarence Theatre, named after the Duke of Clarence who was a regular patron. Following demolition a new theatre on the same site was opened as The Tivoli, but that was not a success and the name was changed again to the Theatre Royal, presenting music hall programmes. At the beginning of the 20th century the name was changed again to the Royal Hippodrome. Three years before the war the theatre came into the ownership of Mr H.R. Armstrong, who attracted some big stars to the theatre that overlooked the Wellington Dock.

Dick Whittamore was employed at the Hippodrome, working his way up from pageboy to assistant manager. His time at the theatre remains some of the happiest days of his life. He recalls that in the spring of 1941 the theatre was concentrating on strip shows, very popular among the hundreds of servicemen stationed in the town. In September that year the famous Evelyn Laye played at the theatre and donated her

£100 salary to local charities. Others topping the bill that year included Ted and Barbara Andrews.

A controversy over a planned Sunday show at the Hippodrome in December 1943 created Fleet Street headlines. The Lord's Day Observance Society intervened and the show had to be cancelled. Comedian Tommy Trinder read about the problem and offered to bring a first-class show to Hellfire Corner Dover that would not infringe the Sunday opening regulations. The packed show ran for three hours and performers included Tommy Trinder, Sonie Hale, Tessie O'Shea, Derek Roy and the Jerry Allen Trio. Dick Whittamore commented, 'Luckily there was no enemy action during the show. The result was a big fat cheque for the Prisoners of War Fund.'

In September 1944 the shelling got so bad that the management decided to close the theatre until life was a little quieter. It was planned to re-open when, in the immediate future, the Canadians captured the German long-range guns. But on Monday 25 September, the day before the final shell, the German gunners dealt their final blow to the theatre which was badly damaged. The Hippodrome never re-opened as a theatre although the bars continued to serve a few customers who ventured along wrecked Snargate Street.

120   *Snargate Street and Hippodrome took a pounding.*

The final chapter came in January 1951 when demolition gangs pulled down the last remaining wall of the theatre, still displaying the proud name The Hippodrome, that had been the venue for so much enjoyment over the years. That wall made a dramatic exit. It collapsed right across Northampton Street (a road that has now disappeared) instead of falling inwards onto the site as intended. A plaque on a wall in Snargate Street still marks the approximate spot where the famous theatre once stood.

Tuesday 26 September 1944 was Dover's final day of shelling as the Canadians gradually captured and smashed the German guns. But that last day brought no relief for it resulted in the most serious onslaught on Dover that the town suffered. The enemy gunners were determined to use up as many shells as possible before their end came.

The real bombardment began at lunch time when for three hours or more German shells rained down on the town in the most terrifying attack since the first shell was fired at Dover in August 1940. Sixty shells found their mark in Dover on that last day and in such a heavy onslaught 10 people lost their lives.

One shell that fell at Broadlees, not far from where Louis Bleriot landed on the first flight across the Channel, killed a Royal Artillery sergeant and injured three other soldiers. Another shell fell on River recreation ground while others fell in the sea.

Later in the day came another three hours of continuous shelling, the first of which sliced through 40 feet of chalk and nine inches of concrete at the entrance to the underground tunnel that ran from Durham Hill to Snargate Street. The debris fell on Patience Ransley, 66, who was dead when dug out.

Throughout the afternoon more shells were shot across the Strait and at one stage a dozen missiles were fired in 14 minutes and a score in half an hour. Four civilians were killed and only three seriously injured. Those who died, in addition to Mrs Ransley, were: Len Edmond, 35, Florence Marsh, 61 and Ethel Cockroft, 72. An RAF officer was killed and five of his team injured, including three WAAF members, when a shell fell close to Dover Grammar School for Girls in Frith Road, being used as the headquarters of the balloon barrage. A naval officer died in Snargate Street and two soldiers were killed at Old Park, while another died from his injuries in hospital.

More than 30 shells fell in a small radius in the centre of the town with the bulk in the Castle estate area. Soldiers and sailors were called out to clear roads of debris and extra police were drafted into Dover from other towns. Half a dozen shells fell in the sea, one near the wreck of HMS *Codrington* that had been beached opposite Waterloo Crescent. One shell that failed to explode went deep into the ground at the back of Victoria Park. Norman Sutton recorded:

> When the All Clear was sounded, the signal was never more welcome for there were few people in Dover who had not been badly shaken by the ordeal. The devastation in the town was great with many roads closed and services cut. There is no doubt that public morale was strained more that day than by any other experienced during the whole of the war.

121   *The last shell – Hubbard's umbrella shop, 26 September 1944.*

The town's ordeal was nearly over and at quarter past seven that evening the last shell fell, not only on Dover but the whole of England. It crashed down on Hubbard's umbrella store at the corner of Castle Street and Church Street near the Market Square (the site is the former TSB bank now used as a local authority centre). Several people were nearby but no one was hurt. Three shops were demolished and two others damaged by this final shell.

During those last 48 hours, as people huddled in their shelters, national newspapers had been publishing news that Dover's ordeal was over. That caused some wry smiles on Dovorian's faces as more shells rained down.

Although the last shell had fallen, the authorities were taking no chances and advised the public to keep under cover – just in case. It was nearly two hours after that last shell before the All Clear sounded.

On that momentous September evening it was not realised that shelling had finally ended. It was just another All Clear and for all the people of Dover knew another shell would come crashing down on their town. Consequently, despite what some elements of the press declared, there were no celebrations that evening.

The people of Dover could hardly believe their ears when, on Saturday 30 September, the mayor announced on the town's loudspeakers that the last shell had been fired. He

had received official information from the
Canadians on the other side of the Channel
that all the guns had been captured and their
surviving crews were now prisoners of war.
Dover could breathe again.

When the news of the end of shelling was
announced the people of the town, mixing
with members of the armed forces, poured
out into the streets. Any available bunting
and flags soon appeared.

Norman Sutton observed: 'There were no
mad scenes. Only sober thankfulness that it was
all over, a thankfulness which found expression
in the following day's church services.'

During that dreadful final September
of shelling there were 41 civilians killed,
67 seriously injured, 158 houses destroyed,
1,500 seriously damaged, 6,750 less seriously
damaged and a dozen highways closed because

122 *Leaving the cave shelters for the last time with the
end of shelling.*

123 *On the Western Heights celebrating the capture of the German guns at Calais.*

124   *Dover's shells and bombs 1940-4.*

of damage. Rescue services attended more than 50 incidents, recovering 23 people alive and 30 bodies.

With the end of shelling enemy action at Dover seemed to be at an end, but there were a few alerts when flying bombs, fired from planes, passed near to the town. Occasionally, a German plane would be in the area searching for Dunkirk, the French port where the enemy still held out.

German one-man submarines were active in the Channel at the end of 1944 and torpedoed several ships near the Goodwin Sands, so Dover harbour lookouts remained alert.

The King and Queen visited Dover on 18 October to provide royal recognition of what Dovorians had been through during their ordeal of bombing and shelling. Peter

125   *King George VI with Mayor Cairns inspects a guard of honour of Dover firewomen.*

126   *Queen Elizabeth accompanied her husband during the 1944 visit.*

Bean remembers the occasion:

> They inspected the civilian services and saw the damage that Dover had suffered during those eventful years. Finally the worst of the war was over for poor old Dover and we, the bank staff, were granted an extra week's holiday for devotion to duty.

So ended 1944, a year that will long remain in the annals of the town.

1945

Peace at Last

THE YEAR BEGAN with national recognition of Dover's mayor throughout the war years, Alderman 'Jimmy' Cairns, when he was awarded the OBE in January.

Dover-based ferries played a major role throughout much of the war. Several, manned by Dover crew members, were sunk with considerable loss of life.

The Southern Railway train ferries, which in peacetime sailed from the ferry dock at the western docks to Dunkirk, were used by the Royal Navy to lay mines in the Channel and elsewhere. The *Hampton*, the *Shepperton* and the *Twickenham* ferries were constructed with strengthened decks in order to carry carriages and wagons in their peacetime role. Inside the train deck were four sets of rails, two of which ran to the stern and these were ideal for laying a large number of mines at speed. Normally minelaying was carried out by Royal Navy ships or fast patrol boats where they were mounted on the decks and dropped over the side to protect the British coast. This was relatively slow work, but the Dover train ferries, with ample space inside to accommodate the mines, were ideal because the mines could be loaded fairly easily rather than being craned onto the other ships.

The trio of train ferries were normally based in the ferry dock where there were facilities for loading the mines. Later, after the *Hampton* and *Shepperton* (known as train ferry A and train ferry B) had moved from Dover the ferry dock was covered in camouflage netting to conceal the MTBs based there.

All three were involved in the evacuation of troops from ports in north-west France, including Le Havre, Brest and St Valery en Caux, before being enlisted as military vehicle ferries between Stranraer and Belfast. The *Shepperton* also assisted in the evacuation of civilians from Jersey in June 1940.

Towards the end of the war the train ferries were back in Dover and were fitted with huge, ugly, stern-lifting gear to enable trains to be off-loaded at Calais and Cherbourg as Allied troops fighting their way through France were in need of rail transport for supplies.

127   *(Above)* Shepperton *ferry.*

128   *(Above right)* Twickenham *ferry.*

129   *(Right)* Invicta *troopship.*

130   Canterbury *before the war.*

More than a thousand railway engines were exported from Dover this way before the end of hostilities and immediately after the war.

Southern Railway's 'posh' *Invicta*, under construction for the Golden Arrow service in 1939, was completed in July 1940 and laid up. She was fitted out in May 1942 as a landing craft for the infantry in readiness for the ill-fated Dieppe Raid. In January 1945 the *Invicta* was engaged in trooping between Tilbury and Ostend and, in May, sailed for Guernsey with liberation troops, before trooping duties between Dover and Calais in October 1945. She entered commercial service at Dover in October 1946.

The day war was declared on 3 September 1939 the Dover-based passenger ferry *Canterbury* carried nearly two thousand troops to Boulogne. *Canterbury* was then taken over by the Admiralty for duties at Southampton, sailing to Brest, Cherbourg and the Hook of Holland. She made five crossings of the Channel to the Dunkirk beaches between 25 May and 3 June 1940, rescuing 5,652 British and French troops. She was then diverted to north-west France for the evacuation of more troops from Le Havre and Brest.

As a landing ship for the infantry the *Canterbury* took part in the Normandy invasion in 1944, putting troops ashore on Juno Beach. In April 1946 she was released for civilian service to restart the Golden Arrow service from Dover in April 1946.

The *Maid of Kent*, built in 1925 and licensed to carry 1,400 passengers during its peacetime career, was brought into military service soon after the outbreak of the war. In September 1939

131   Canterbury *during the war.*

the ship was carrying the BEF to France before being converted into a hospital ship at Southampton and it began operating between Newhaven and Dieppe.

John Hendy, a former Dover man who is an authority on Channel ferries, recalled:

The *Maid of Kent* arrived at Dieppe during the evening of 18 May in 1940 and had been there less than an hour when nine bombs fell near her. There were more air raids the following night so the master requested permission to move the ship from the inner harbour to tidal berths to allow a swifter escape if necessary.

132   Maid of Kent *as a hospital ship.*

Permission was granted but the lock gates became jammed and there is the suspicion this was the result of sabotage. A further air attack followed that same evening and the ship was hit aft, one bomb entering the engine room causing a fire which spread. The ship had to be abandoned. Nine of the personnel on board were killed.

The *Isle of Thanet* was also engaged in transporting the BEF to France, via Southampton, and was also converted to a hospital ship. She took part in Operation Dynamo on 25 May on her first trip, but after that failed twice to reach Dunkirk because of heavy shelling from the enemy-captured coast. She was then in collision with the *Reward* (a Dover-based examination vessel), which sank. The *Isle of Thanet* was itself badly damaged and forced to retire to Newhaven for repairs.

Following these repairs, the former Dover ferry sailed for the Irish Sea and was fitted out as a Fleet Air Arm target vessel before taking part in Operation Neptune as an infantry landing ship and an assault group headquarter vessel operating off Juno Beach during the D-Day invasion. She later became a headquarters ship off Gold Beach on the Normandy beachhead. Towards the end of the war the *Isle of Thanet* was engaged in carrying troops between Southampton and Ostend before being released to return to commercial service.

Another local ferry was the *Biarritz*, the only local railway-owned ship to serve throughout both world wars. She also carried BEF troops to France in September 1939 and then sailed to Rotterdam to evacuate British residents as the enemy advanced across the Low Countries. *Biarritz* took part in the evacuation of Dunkirk (Operation Dynamo) and on 27 May sailed

133   *The* Biarritz.

134   Autocarrier.

from Dover. She was hit four times by shells fired from the coast near Calais and was so damaged she returned to Dover with two crew injured. After repairs the ship took part in the evacuation from the Channel Islands and from north-west France. During the D-Day invasion the ferry became a reserve landing ship.

The *Maid of Orleans*, another local ferry and sister to the *Biarritz*, also had an eventful war. At one time one of her passengers was Prime Minister Winston Churchill, ferrying him on the Clyde to the *Queen Mary*.

The *Maid* was damaged off Dover in January 1940 when in collision with the pilot vessel *Prudence*. Repaired, she was sent to Rotterdam in case she was needed to evacuate British subjects, and two months later carried Guardsmen to the Hook of Holland to fight a rearguard action. During September and October 1940 she operated to the Isle of Man carrying alien and British internees.

She also took part in Operation Dynamo off the Dunkirk Beaches and after six Channel crossings was rammed by the destroyer HMS *Worcester* and forced to retire to Southampton. In June 1944 the *Maid* carried commandos to land on Sword Beach during the Normandy

135   Forde.

invasion and later made more Channel crossings to land troops at Juno Beach. On 28 June while returning from the invasion beaches she hit a mine and sank in 30 minutes.

The car carrier *Autocarrier*, another ferry that pre-war operated out of Dover, also took part in Operation Dynamo in 1940, making two sailings to Dunkirk before being diverted to Southampton for the evacuation of people from the Channel Islands. She was then converted to a welfare ship based at Scapa Flow until the end of the war.

Local railway-owned cargo ships *Deal*, *Tonbridge* and *Whitstable* also had honourable war careers. The *Deal* assisted in the evacuation of St Malo in 1940 and was then used as a barrage balloon vessel in the Thames estuary and the Solent. The *Tonbridge* assisted in the evacuation of Guernsey in 1940 before being converted to a net layer. She was bombed and sank in six minutes off Great Yarmouth in August 1941 when 32 members of the crew were lost. The *Whitstable* took part in Operation Dynamo, rescuing soldiers from Bray east of Dunkirk, the evacuation of the Channel Islands and finally transporting milk between Larne and Stranraer.

Townsend Brothers' ferry *Forde*, in peacetime sailing between Dover's Eastern Docks and Calais, spent the war years as a naval salvage vessel.

No more enemy bombs or shells fell on Dover in 1945 as the long war dragged to its close. The delight of peaceful days and nights was only upset by the news that HM Telegraph ship

136   *Troops embarking for France.*

137   *Helping the wounded ashore.*

Alert, almost completely manned by Dover men, was sunk by enemy action on 24 February off the Isle of Thanet.

One of the most sombre places in Dover during the 1939-45 war was the special mortuary where a small housing estate has now been built. The then quarry and limekiln site just off Tower Street, Tower Hamlets, was where many of Dover's dead were taken, as were the bodies of Allied soldiers and Germans, some recovered from the Channel.

Mr George Baggaley, the mortuary superintendent, dealt with the bodies of 734 victims of war. At the war's end these were revealed as: 478 members of the armed forces (including 201 from Dunkirk), 35 Merchant Navy seafarers, 201 civilians and 20 aliens including Germans.

There were two cottages backed up against the chalk cliff and it was here that the task of identifying the dead was carried out. Two caves dug into the cliff provided a cool Chapel of Rest.

After the Germans had been driven from the French coast and their E-boat fleet, based on the Belgian coast, was driven away, Dover became a busy port. Hundreds of troops and war material were shipped from the port for the continent as the allies advanced towards Germany. Amphibious craft passed through Dover on the way to the troops preparing to cross the Rhine. Dover seafront, including Granville Gardens, was often jammed with tanks so that some had to be parked on bombed sites in Townwall Street and the St James' area.

Enemy submarines still lurked in the Channel and Dovorians often heard the explosions of mines and depth charges. The alert was sounded occasionally as flying bombs, launched from German piloted aircraft, crossed the coast. One was brought down in the sea off Sandwich and another passed over Canterbury. Dover's last alert was sounded at 10 p.m. on 25 March.

Huge armadas of Allied aircraft, some towing gliders, flew over Dover on their way to assist in the crossing of the Rhine. Germany was in a state of collapse, Hitler had committed suicide and on 8 May the town celebrated Victory in Europe Day (VE Day).

The loud speakers erected to give warning of shelling were used to broadcast Prime Minister Churchill's victory speech and throughout the day the speakers provided music for dancing in the gaily decorated streets.

As darkness fell a crowd of soldiers, sailors, an occasional American serviceman and Dover teenagers lit a huge bonfire in the Market Square with the flames fed by wood from the many damaged properties in the locality. Barry Fincham joined in the celebrations. He remembers:

May 8th 1945. Victory at last with Germany having to accept unconditional surrender. Jubilation all over the town. There was a huge bonfire on the beach with plenty of wood from war damaged property to keep the flames going. Then we had Buckland church choir singing in a massed church service in Charlton Church to celebrate Victory in Europe. German prisoners of war started working in the town, digging a large trench up London Road and Old Park Road to install a new drainage system. They were unguarded and seemed a sullen down-trodden lot. Many housewives gave them tea and showed them sympathy.

138 *VE Day party, Clarendon Street.*

The first boats carrying soldiers on leave arrived at Dover in January 1945 and throughout the year there was a steady stream of military personnel placed in transit camps at Old Park Barracks, at the Duke of York's Royal Military School and at the former Oil Mills in Limekiln Street. A Canadian transit camp was established at Connaught Barracks. With thousands of soldiers passing through Dover, either on leave or being demobbed, a large NAAFI was opened in a Nissen hut in the Market Square. It was capable of accommodating 1,500 members of the armed forces.

To find homes to replace the hundreds wrecked by enemy action, in March Dover council accepted 159 American prefabricated houses to be placed on the outskirts of the town (now Buckland Estate, then a farm) and at Randolph Road (destroyed by a parachute mine). Another 238 British prefabs were also ordered for the Buckland Valley site. During 1945 around a thousand building workers, including Belgian volunteers, were engaged in repairing war-damaged homes in the town.

Shakespeare Beach (the Western Beach) was re-opened to bathers in the spring and by Easter the seafront was largely cleared of its wartime obstructions. The Ostend ferry service, suspended in May 1940, restarted on 23 October 1945, but sailings were from Folkestone on a temporary basis and not from Dover.

Some industry began returning to Dover. A licence was granted to Dover Engineering Works for partial rebuilding in Charlton Green following serious bomb and shell damage. The works were evacuated to Watford in 1940, under government direction, where major war production was carried out, including building part of the Mulberry Harbour, used in the 1944 Normandy invasion.

Wiggins, Teape paper mills at Buckland and Crabble also returned in 1945, following repairs from war damage, but Chitty's shell-destroyed flour mill at Charlton Green was never rebuilt and many jobs were lost as a result. Dover Borough Council considered applying for

139 *A prefab(ricated) house.*

140   *VJ Day.*

a compulsory purchase order for the site of the mill and neighbouring land for industry. One result was the construction of factory premises in Charlton Green for Portland Plastics, used much later as a Royal Mail sorting office.

A number of voluntary organisations that had provided valuable services during the raids 'stood down'. These included the central organisation of the Women's Voluntary Service which, under Mrs Beeston, had carried out many duties under shellfire since 1940. The part-time volunteers in the Civil Defence and National Fire Service were released from their duties with thanks. The St John Ambulance had provided many of the Civil Defence first aid workers during the raids.

Dover's Home Guard 'stood down' earlier in November 1944, although remained on the reserve until officially disbanded. Allan Edgington was in the army cadets at a time when the Home Guard was still active. His father was in the Home Guard and when they had .303 firing practice at Lydden Spout Allan was 'recruited' to man the butts to signal if the riflemen were on target. Recalls Allan: 'When they had Bren gun or Sten gun practice, carried out in one of the moats of the Western Heights, they often let us have a go.'

A second phase of the Home Guard was later established in Dover and the villages during the 'Cold War.'

141   *Ration books.*

The Prince of Wales Pier, Southern Breakwater and Eastern Arm, all prohibited areas during the conflict, were re-opened to anglers in August 1945. But, at that stage, the Admiralty Pier remained closed to the public.

When, on 15 August, Victory against Japan (VJ Day) was celebrated there was another bonfire in the Market Square which was so fierce that it burnt a hole in the tarmac. There was another on the seafront. The *Dover Express* reported: 'Considerable damage was caused by seizure of anything combustible including seats from the seafront promenade.'

When the town's official celebrations were organised the authorities ensured the town's bonfire would be well away from the centre of Dover. A 30ft-high bonfire was built on Whinless Down and was lit by the mayor, Councillor Bill Fish. It was his last official act. Mr Fish died the next day from a seizure.

Even when the war was over strict food rationing remained in force and the winter of 1945-6 was severe and fuel was hard to come by. The council ripped up all the hardwood blocks from the roads, where they remained in parts of the town, and these provided a much-needed heating source for many Dover families.

EPILOGUE

Here was respect throughout much of the 'free world' for the way Dover, Britain's front line town, had withstood the ravages of enemy bombs and shells for so long. But Dover and its people faced an uphill task to readjust to peacetime. As those who had evacuated returned to Dover there was the massive task of rehousing around 1,300 families where hundreds of homes lay in ruins.

It was not long before there was dissension over the future shape of Dover. The old regime of Dover Borough Council was swept away and, for the first time, Labour was in control. The new authority wanted a modern Dover. Those whose homes, shops and workplaces were to be swept away by compulsory purchase, were opposed. So were those who did not want a 75 ft-wide highway driven through the main street. Money was short, the nation was nearly bankrupt and many of the schemes came to nothing.

Wartime defence posts (pill boxes) and other anti-invasion structures on the seafront and elsewhere were demolished and the Royal Navy base in Dover closed down.

County cricket restarted in Dover with Kent taking the honours over both Glamorgan and Derbyshire. The Golden Arrow service to the continent recommenced through Dover in 1946 and the first liner, a Royal Netherlands' ship, called at the port again.

One aspect of the worldwide recognition of the bravery of Dover's wartime population was the launch of an international appeal for £250,000 to build a Battle of Britain hospital on the white cliffs of Dover. Money quickly poured in and Queen Elizabeth agreed to be patron. Then came the decision of the Labour government to bring in the National Health Service that would take over the nation's hospitals. As a result the appeal fund was wound up and much of the money was spent on providing the Battle of Britain homes, facing York Street, for senior citizens.

One happy event in Dover was the installation of Sir Winston Churchill in 1946 as Lord Warden of the Cinque Ports.

142   *Woolcomber Street's war-damaged houses awaiting demolition in 1947.*

143   *Marine Parade pre-war.*

144   *Marine Parade post-war.*

145   *Basketball in the remains of Granville Gardens.*

146   *A post-war plan for Dover that never materialised.*

Dover never really recovered from the hammering it received during the 1939-45 war. The population, more than 40,000 before September 1939, only increased to 33,000, even after the return of evacuees, both adults and children, and stands at around 30,000 today.

The attractive sweep of houses on the seafront, from Granville Gardens to Douro Place, was never rebuilt. Before the war a number had provided bed-and-breakfast guest house accommodation for the town's annual holiday-makers. The Royal Cinque Ports Yacht Club was also situated there. Much of this site is now occupied by the flats of The Gateway.

Several churches, once offering proud architecture, suffered the ravages of war and have since been torn down, some to match the smaller population.

Let Barry Fincham tell of the long-lasting effects that many Dovorians suffered for years after the war:

> Even after 60 years I still feel my stomach turn over when a low flying aircraft goes overhead. And any sudden loud explosion causes my heart to miss a beat. For those who suffered, war leaves permanent scars.
>
> Dover had the heart ripped out of it and has never recovered. There was never any money available from governments or from private investment to restructure the town back to its pre-war elegance and character. Old much-damaged properties were demolished and cheap, colourless buildings, lacking any form of character, were substituted in their place.

Some scars left behind after four years of bombing and shelling can still be seen with the occasional empty site, bombed sites as they were called, with ugly plastered sides of buildings showing where the adjacent war-damaged property was demolished.

Sir Patrick Abercrombie's plan for a 'new Dover', published in 1946, envisaged the reconstruction of much of the town in the Dour valley over the next 20 years. It never happened.

BIBLIOGRAPHY

Baxter, G., *Aircraft Casualties in Kent* (1990)

Bates, W., *My Life* (unpublished)

Cook, R., *Shellfire Corner Carries On* (1942)

Dover Express, various (1939-2002)

Foster, R., *Dover Front* (1941)

Friend, D., *Field of Human Conflict* (1990)

Gray, B., *Sunday Pictorial* (1940)

Harman, J., *My Dover* (2001)

Hayward, P., *Children in Exile* (1997)

Hewitt, J., *Greetings, Dover!* (2002)

Humphreys, R., *Dover at War* (1993)

Kent Messenger, various (1940-90)

Kershaw, R., *Never Surrender* (2009)

Russell, A., BBC broadcast (1944)

Vulyak, C., *Dover Society Newsletter* (2009)

Whittamore, D., *Collected Memories of a Century* (2000)

INDEX

Unfortunately, while a considerable number of those killed and injured in Dover are named in the text, it was not possible to include them in the index.

Page numbers in **bold** refer to illustration captions.